RAKESH BANSAL, a post graduate in International Business Management, grew interested in the stock market in 1998 and is now a full time trader. He is a result driven professional with nearly two decades of rich experience in the areas of technical analysis, wealth management, investment analysis and portfolio management. He is currently an expert panelist with Zee Business where he regularly shares his market outlook and trading picks.

Rakesh Bansal's popular first book — *Profitable Short Term Trading Strategies* — is also published by Vision Books.

Rakesh Bansal is active on Twitter and his Twitter handle is @iamrakeshbansal. He can also be reached at rakesh1973@yahoo.com.

Also by
Rakesh Bansal

~

Profitable Short-Term Trading Strategies

~

PROFITABLE ELLIOTT WAVE TRADING STRATEGIES

RAKESH
BANSAL

www.visionbooksindia.com

www.visionbooksindia.com

Disclaimer

The author and the publisher disclaim all legal or other responsibilities for any losses which investors may suffer by investing or trading using the methods described in this book. Readers are advised to seek professional guidance before making any specific investments. This book is meant purely for the purpose of investor and trader education.

First Published, 2020
Reprinted, 2021, 2024

A Vision Books Original

ISBN 10: 93-86268-37-X
ISBN 13: 978-93-86268-37-2

Published by
Vision Books Pvt. Ltd.
(Incorporating Orient Paperbacks and CARING imprints)
24 Feroze Gandhi Road, Lajpat Nagar 3
New Delhi 110024, India.
Phone: (+91-11) 2984 0821 / 22
e-mail: visionbooks@gmail.com

Printed at
Thomson Press
B-315, Okhla Industrial Area, Phase 1
New Delhi 110020, India.

Dedication

SMT. SUDARSHAN BANSAL

This book is dedicated to my mother,
Smt. Sudarshan Bansal, my hero.

She is by far the strongest woman I have ever known.

No words are sufficient to describe my mother's contribution to my life. I owe every bit of my existence to her. She is the bones of my spine, keeping me straight and true.

Men are what their mothers make them and home is where your mother is.

Contents

~

Preface

~

This book is all about using Elliott Wave Theory for profitable trading.

Each chapter in the book presents information in a logical, sequential fashion. The material in each chapter is built upon the information presented in the preceding chapters. The reader should therefore proceed chapter-wise, from the beginning to the end, in order to clearly grasp the underlying logic of the profitable Elliott Wave trading strategies presented in this book. Each and every topic is thereafter explained in detail, with numerous real examples from the Indian markets.

Making money in the stock market is never easy since "money is the reward for being right in the market." In this book, I have attempted to explain how Elliott Wave Theory could help you be "right in the market" and make money through profitable stock market trading.

~

1

Introduction to Elliott Wave Theory

Elliott Wave Theory is based on the hypothesis that stock prices move due to the combined, fluctuating optimism and pessimism of all market participants. Such swings in the participants' sentiment make stock prices move in certain repetitive patterns, or trends. Elliott Wave Theory places these trends in two categories as follows:

1. Dominant trend, which is a 5-wave pattern; and
2. Corrective trend, which is a 3-wave pattern.

Elliott Wave Theory holds that within each of these two trends, stock prices alternate between impulsive and corrective waves — and the theory forecasts market trends by identifying extremes in investor sentiment and psychology.

Dominant Trend — 5-Wave Pattern

The dominant trend is basically a move in the direction of the main trend and it's a 5-wave pattern. Thus:

- In rising markets when stock prices are going up, the dominant trend is a 5-wave pattern in the upward direction.
- In declining markets when stock prices are going down, the dominant trend is a 5-wave pattern in the downward direction.

Characteristics of the Dominant Trend When Markets are Rising

- **Wave 1** is usually a weak rally.

- **Wave 2** is a sell-off once Wave 1 is over. Wave 2 never goes below the starting point of Wave 1.
- **Wave 3** is a strong rally which suggests that most market participants are convinced about the rally's strength.
- **Wave 4** is, unmistakably, a correction.
- **Wave 5** is the last wave of the dominant trend, after which the market tops out and thereafter enters a new phase.

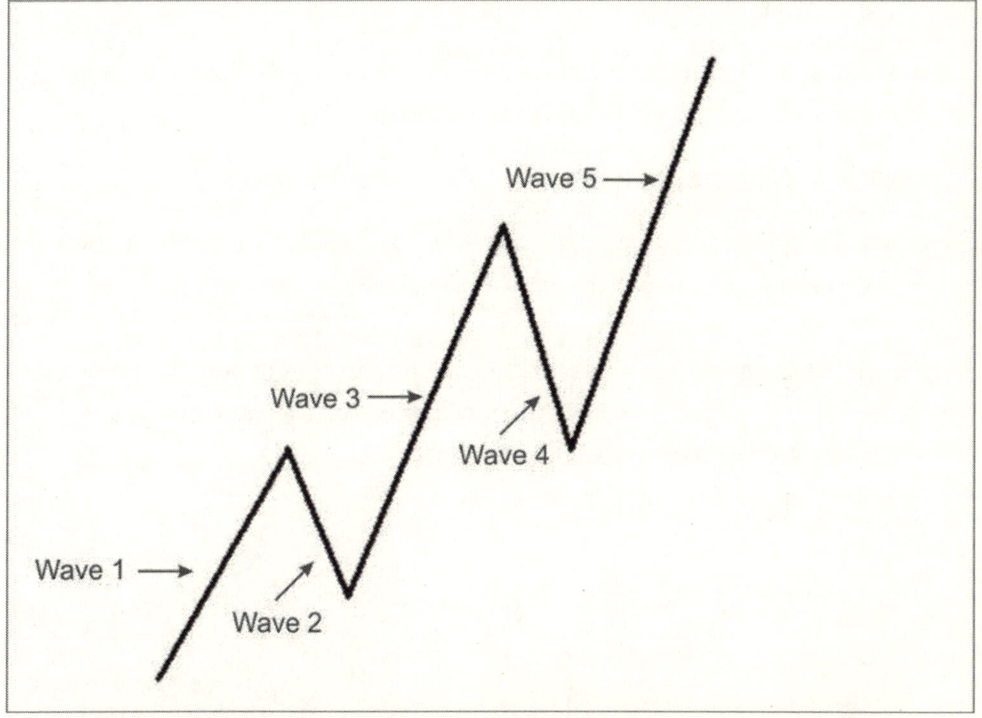

Figure 1.1: **The 5-wave sequence of an Elliott Wave dominant trend in a rising market. Waves 1, 3 and 5 are impulsive waves; waves 2 and 4 are corrective waves**

~

Figure 1.1 illustrates the sequence of a rising 5-wave dominant trend. Here, Wave 1, Wave 3 and Wave 5 are impulsive waves, while Wave 2 and Wave 4 are corrective waves.

Characteristics of the Dominant Trend When Markets are Declining

- **Wave 1** is usually a weak correction.
- **Wave 2** indicates a strong pullback rally but it never rises beyond the starting point of Wave 1.
- **Wave 3** is a strong down move as most market participants are now convinced about the trend of the price move.
- **Wave 4** is clearly a pullback.
- **Wave 5** is the last wave of the dominant trend, after which the market bottoms out and thereafter enters a new phase.

Figure 1.2 illustrates the 5-wave sequence of a declining dominant trend. Here, Wave 1, Wave 3 and Wave 5 are impulsive waves, while Wave 2 and Wave 4 are corrective waves.

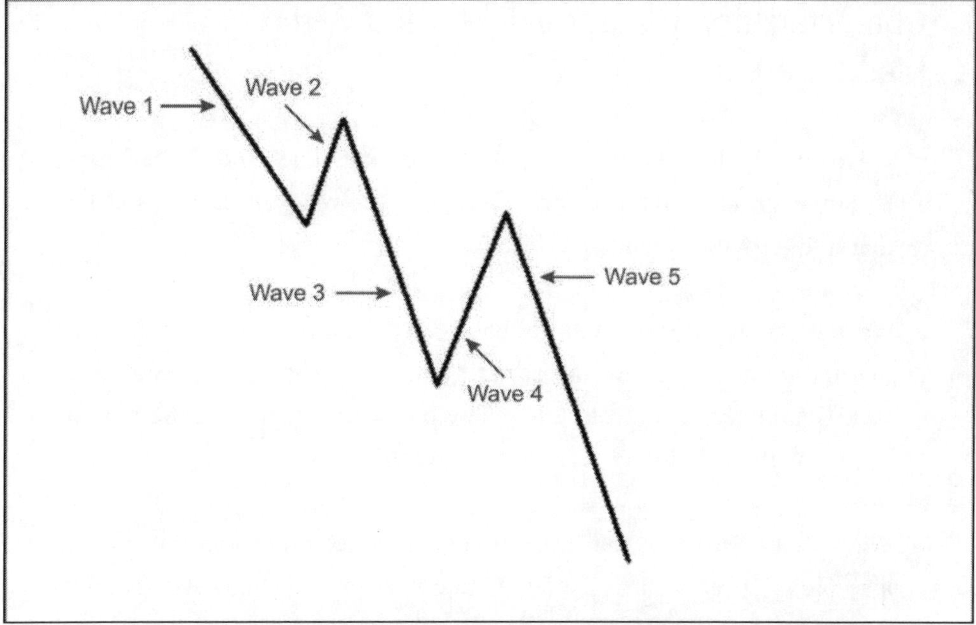

Figure 1.2: **The 5-wave sequence of an Elliott Wave dominant trend when markets are declining. Waves 2 and 4 are corrective waves; waves 1, 3 and 5 are impulsive waves**

~

Corrective Trend — 3-Wave Pattern

The corrective trend is basically a move against the direction of the dominant trend. It's a 3-wave pattern, as follows:

- In rising markets when the dominant trend is up, the corrective trend is a 3-wave pattern in the downward direction;
- In falling markets when the main dominant is down, the corrective trend is a 3-wave pattern in the upward direction.

Characteristics of a Corrective Trend When Markets are Rising

- **Wave A** is the beginning of a new bear market. The fundamental news is, however, still positive and few people are ready to accept the fact that market will now decline.

- **Wave B** is basically a small pullback rally which gives the impression that the upmove has resumed after a break and that the bull run is intact. Usually, prices fail to make new highs and, typically, the volume during Wave B is lower than that during Wave A.

- **Wave C:** In Wave C, the price again starts declining and the volume also picks up. It's during Wave C that everyone realises that the market decline is likely to continue and so the number of market participation on the sell side increases.

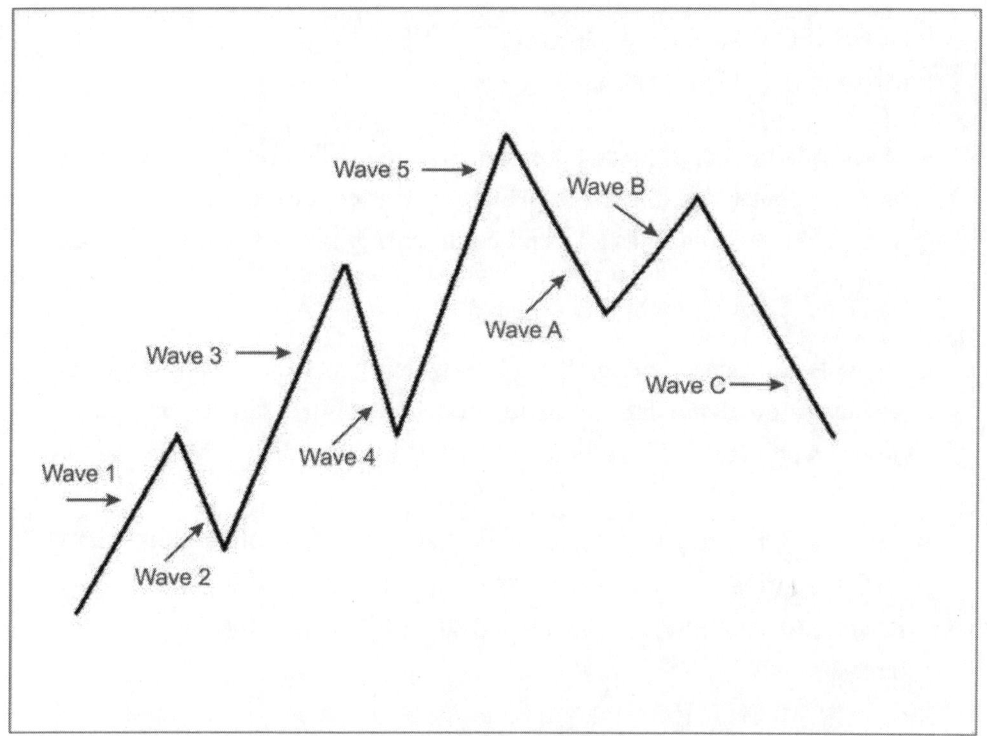

Figure 1.3: **Elliott Wave corrective trend — a 3-wave correction — when markets are rising. Waves A and C are impulsive waves while Wave B is a corrective wave.**

~

Figure 1.3 illustrates a 3-wave downward corrective pattern.

Here, after a market rally in a basic 5-wave sequence, a market top is made and the market thereafter enters a new phase, namely the 3-wave downward corrective phase illustrated by waves A, B and C shown in Figure 1.3.

In Figure 1.3, waves 1, 3, 5, A and C are impulsive waves, whereas waves 2, 4 and B are corrective waves.

Characteristics of a Corrective Trend When Markets are Declining

- **Wave A** is the beginning of a new bull market. The fundamental news is still negative at this stage, which is why nobody is quite ready to accept the fact that market trend could change from down to up from here on.

- **Wave B** is basically a small decline which gives the feeling that the earlier original fall has resumed. Prices, however, fail to make new lows and typically the volume in Wave B is lower than in Wave A.

- **Wave C:** The price now again starts rising and the volume also picks up. It's during Wave C that everyone accepts the likelihood of a trend change to up — hence the market participation on the buy side increases.

Figure 1.4 illustrates the 3-wave upward corrective wave sequence that indicates a change in the dominant trend from down to up.

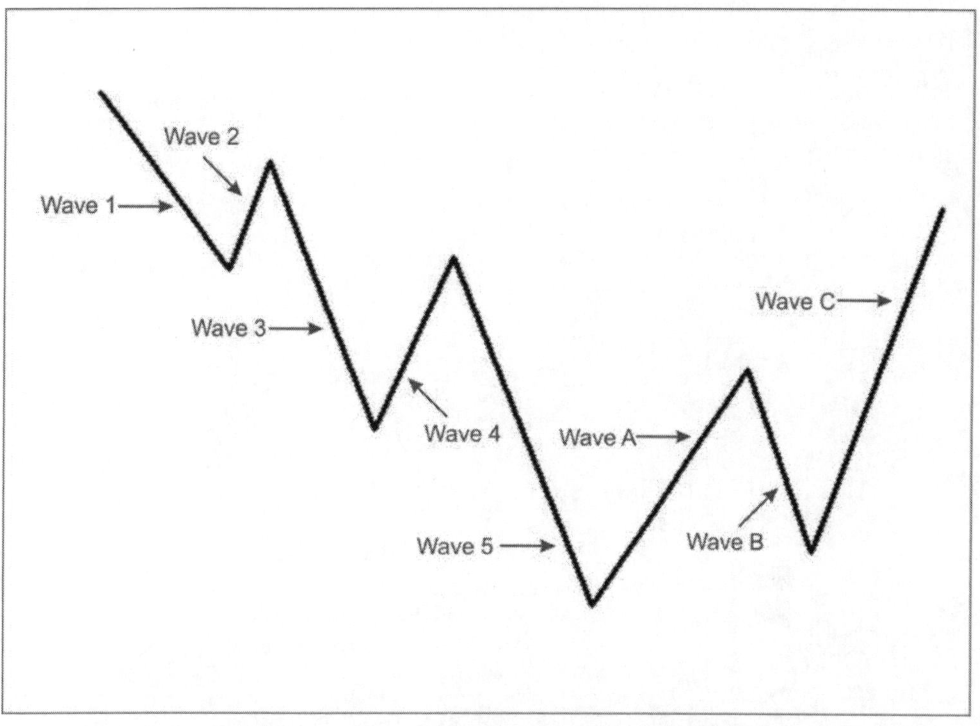

Figure 1.4: **The 3-wave corrective trend when markets are declining; waves A and C are impulsive waves, Wave B is a corrective wave.**

~

In the case of Figure 1.4, a market bottom is made after the market declines in a basic 5-wave sequence. The market then enters a new phase, i.e. a 3-wave upward corrective phase, comprising waves A, B and C.

In this case, waves 1, 3, 5, A and C are all impulsive waves, while waves 2, 4 and B are corrective waves.

~

2

Fractals

As discussed in Chapter 1, Elliott Wave Theory suggests that all dominant trends are subdivided into five smaller waves, while all corrective trends are subdivided into three smaller waves. Accordingly, an Elliott Wave is a fractal. Fractals are self-repeating patterns appearing at every degree of a trend.

Accordingly to Investopedia, "Elliott recognized the 'fractal' nature of markets, and so he was able to break down and analyse them in much greater detail. Fractals are mathematical structures, which on an ever-smaller scale infinitely repeat themselves. Elliott discovered stock index price patterns were structured in the same way. He then began to look at how these repeating patterns could be used as predictive indicators of future market moves."

Impulsive and Corrective Waves when the Main Trend is Up

Figure 2.1 illustrates impulsive and corrective waves when stock prices are rallying, i.e. when the main trend is up.

Waves 1, 3, 5, A and C are impulsive waves and are further subdivided into 5-wave sequences while waves 2, 4 and B are corrective waves which are further subdivided into 3-wave sequences.

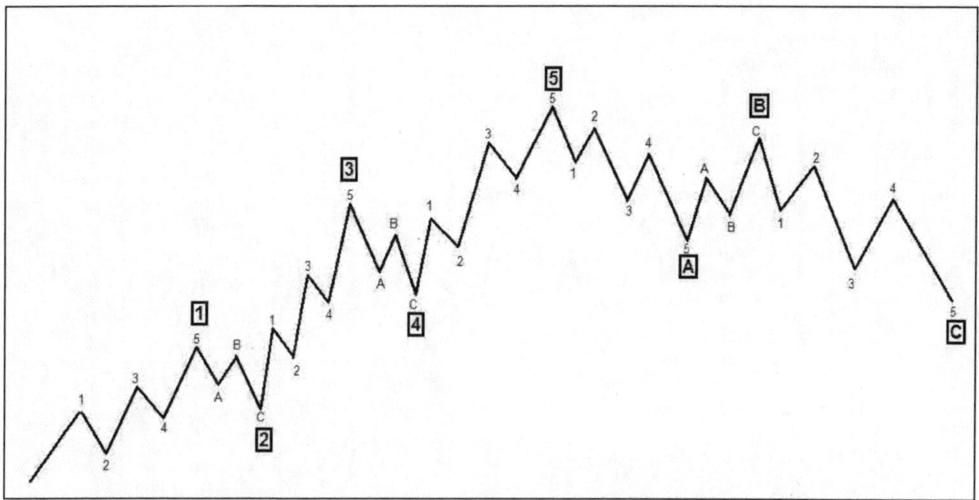

Figure 2.1: **Waves 1, 3, and 5 are impulsive waves within a dominant up trend. Waves A and C are corrective waves during a dominant down trend. All impulsive waves can be subdivided into 5-wave sequences. Corrective waves 2, 4, and B are all corrective waves which can be subdivided into 3-wave sequences**

~

Impulsive and Corrective Waves When the Main Trend is Down

Figure 2.2 illustrates the impulsive and corrective waves when stock prices are declining, i.e. when the main trend is down.

In this case:

- Waves 1, 3, 5, A and C are impulsive waves, further subdivided into a 5-wave sequences; and
- Waves 2, 4 and B are corrective waves, further subdivided into a 3-wave sequenced.

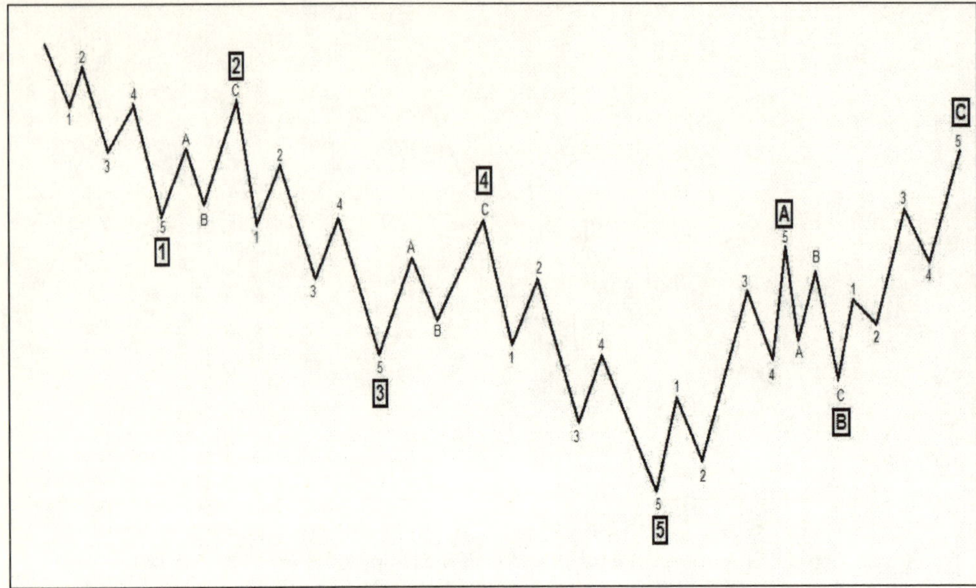

Figure 2.2: **Impulsive waves 1, 3, 5, A and C further subdivide into 5-wave sequences. Corrective waves 2, 4 and B further subdivide into 3-wave sequences.**

~

Significance of Fractals

Fractals enable and simplify the recognition of Elliott Wave patterns and count which, in turn, are the backbone of trading with Elliott Wave theory.

~

3

Rules and Guidelines for Trading Elliott Waves

Rules for Trading Elliott Waves

There are basically three essential rules of Elliott waves.

- **Rule 1:** Wave 2 cannot retrace more than 100% of Wave 1. Otherwise, something is wrong with the wave count.
- **Rule 2:** Wave 3 is always longer than the other two waves, namely Wave 1 and Wave 2, both length wise and time wise
- **Rule 3:** Wave 4 can never overlap Wave 1.

These seemingly simple rules are a crucial, indispensable part of Elliott Wave Theory and you will realise their significance as we proceed further in this book.

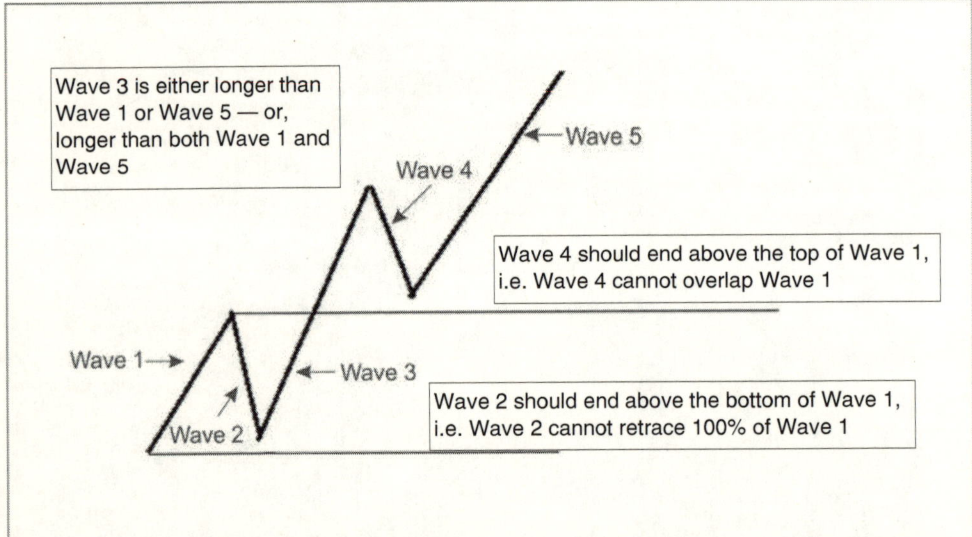

Figure 3.1: **Elliott Wave rules in rising markets**

~

Figure 3.1 illustrates how Elliot wave rules apply in a rising market:

- Wave 2 has not retraced more than 100% of Wave 1;
- Wave 3 is not the shortest wave;
- The up move of Wave 4 ends before the top of Wave 1, i.e. Wave 4 is not overlapping Wave 1.

~

Figure 3.2 illustrates how Elliott Wave rules apply in a falling market:

- Wave 2 has not retraced more than 100% of Wave 1.
- Wave 3 is not the shortest wave.
- The up move of Wave 4 ends below the bottom of Wave 1. In other words, Wave 4 is not overlapping Wave 1.

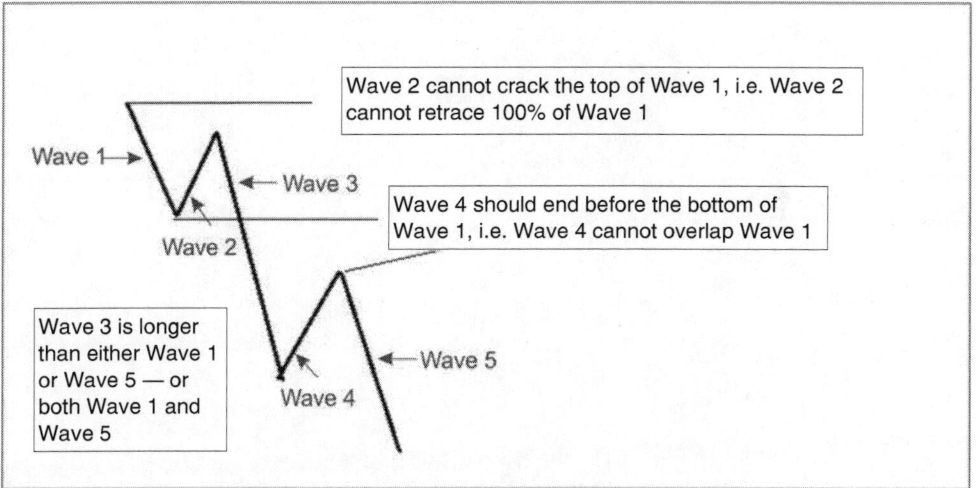

Figure 3.2: **Elliott Wave rules when markets are declining**

~

Guidelines for Trading Elliott Waves

- **Guideline 1:** When Wave 3 is the longest wave, then Wave 5 is usually equal in length to Wave 1.

- **Guideline 2:** The nature of Wave 2 and Wave 4 corrections are contrary to each other. In other words, if Wave 2 is a vicious (sharp) sell off, then Wave 4 would be a flat correction. If, on the other hand, Wave 2 is a flat correction then Wave 4 could be a vicious (sharp) sell off.

- **Guideline 3:** The 3-wave corrective pattern, comprising waves A, B and C after a five-wave dominant pattern (waves 1, 2, 3, 4 and 5) ends prior to the end of Wave 4 of the dominant trend.

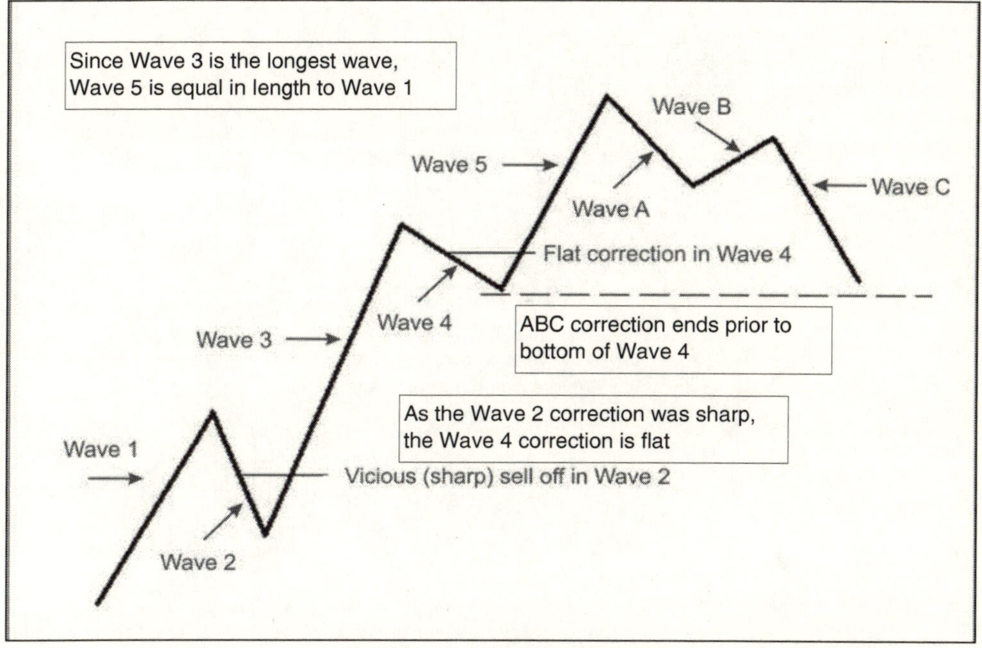

Figure 3.3: **The three Elliott Wave guidelines when Wave 2 is a sharp correction in a rising market**

~

Figure 3.3 illustrates how the three Elliott Wave guidelines work out when Wave 2 is a sharp correction in a rising market:

- Wave 2 is a sharp correction; while Wave 4 is a flat correction.
- Wave 3 is the longest wave; while Wave 5 is equal in length to Wave 1.
- The corrective Wave C ends prior to the bottom of Wave 4.

~

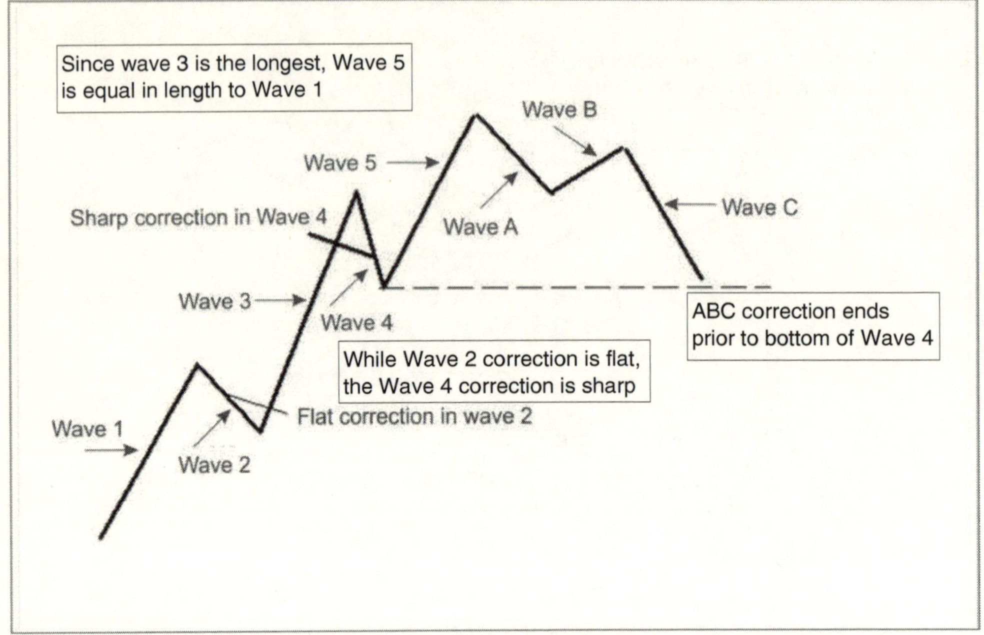

Figure 3.4: **The three Elliott Wave guidelines at work when Wave 2 is a flat correction in a rising market**

~

Figure 3.4 illustrates how the three Elliott Wave guidelines work out when Wave 2 is a flat correction in a rising market:

- Wave 2 is a flat correction; hence Wave 4 is a sharp correction.
- Wave 3 is the longest of the waves while Wave 5 is equal in length to Wave 1.
- The corrective Wave C ends prior to the bottom of Wave 4.

~

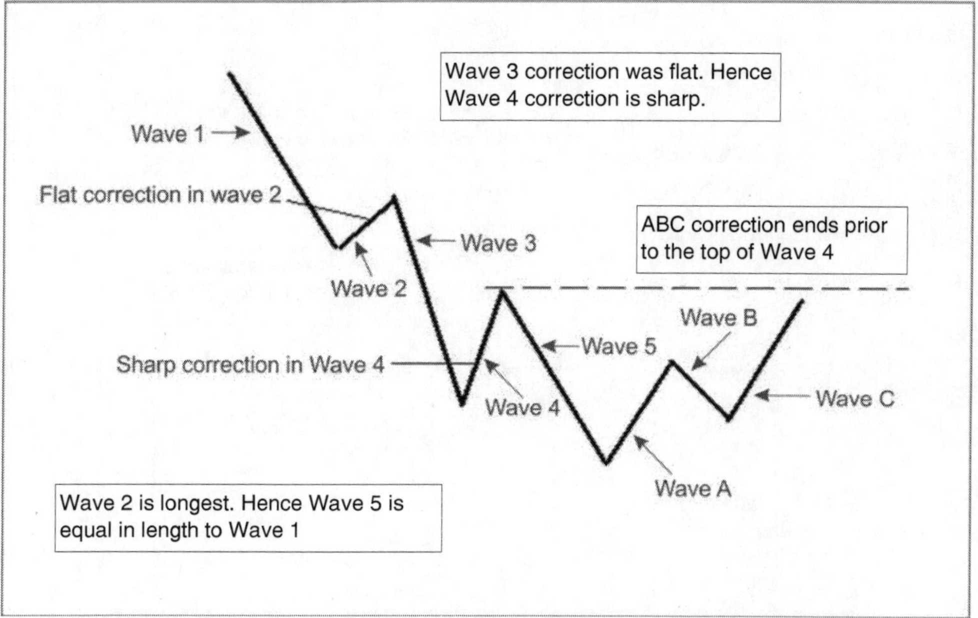

Figure 3.5: **The three Elliott Wave guidelines when Wave 2 is a relatively flat pullback in a falling market**

~

Figure 3.5 illustrates how the three Elliott Wave guidelines work out when Wave 2 is a relatively flat pullback in a falling market:

- Wave 2 is a flat pullback, while Wave 4 is sharp pullback.
- Wave 3 is the longest wave, and Wave 5 is equal in length to Wave 1.
- The corrective Wave C ends prior to the bottom of Wave 4.

~

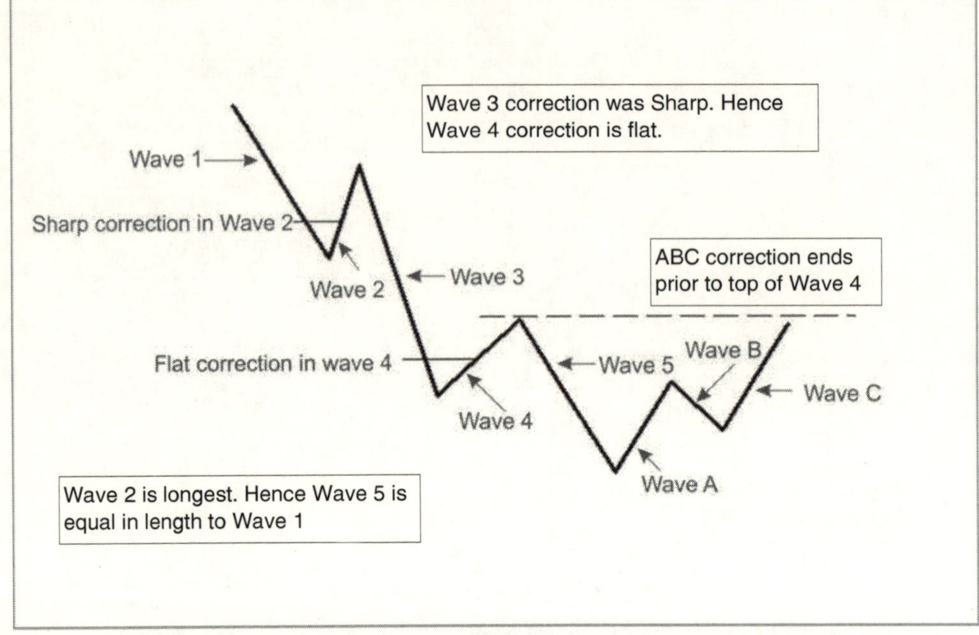

Figure 3.6: **How the three Elliott Wave guidelines work out when Wave 2 is a sharp pullback in a falling market**

~

Figure 3.6 illustrates how the three Elliott Wave guidelines work out when Wave 2 is a sharp pullback in a falling market:

- Wave 2 is a sharp pullback; hence Wave 4 is flat correction.
- Wave 3 is the longest wave, hence Wave 5 is equal in length to Wave 1.
- The corrective Wave C ends prior to the bottom of Wave 4.

~

4

Fibonacci Sequence, Golden Ratio and Fibonacci Retracements

Fibonacci Sequence

The Fibonacci sequence is the series of numbers, 0, 1, 1, 2, 3, 5, 8, 13, 21, 34, and so on.

In this sequence, each successive number is arrived at by adding up the two numbers before it. For example:

- The number 2 is arrived at by adding the two numbers before it in the sequence, i.e. by adding 1+1.
- The number 3 is arrived at by adding the two numbers before it, i.e. by adding 1+2.
- The number 5 in the sequence is arrived at by adding the two numbers before it, i.e. by adding 2+3.
- The next number in the sequence would be 21+34 = 55, and so on.

The Fibonacci sequence is used in many fields, including the stock market. For stock market trading, one basically needs to know only the most common elements of Fibonacci sequences, Fibonacci multiples and Fibonacci ratios.

Fibonacci Multiples

1, 1.618, 2.618, 4.23, 6.85 are all Fibonacci multiples. These multiples are used for identifying Wave 3 and Wave 5 targets.

Fibonacci Ratios

0.14, 0.25, 0.38, 0.5, 0.618 are Fibonacci ratios. These ratios are used for identifying Wave 2 and Wave 4 targets.

Golden Ratio

In mathematics — and in the arts — a ratio is considered golden if the ratio of the sum of two quantities to the larger quantity is equal to the ratio of the larger quantity to the smaller quantity.

Let's understand this with the help of an example.

Let's say there are two quantities. A and B, where A is larger than B.

- If (A + B) ÷ A = A ÷ B, then it is a golden ratio, whose value is 1.6180339887…
- Now, if you take the ratio of any two successive Fibonacci numbers, the answer is very close to the golden ratio, 1.618034.
- In practice, the bigger in value the pair of Fibonacci numbers are, closer is the approximation of their ratio to the golden ratio.

Significance of the Golden Ratio

The golden ratio appears frequently in stock markets, typically close to the levels where wave tops and bottoms get formed. **The golden ratio, therefore, helps in identifying key turning points of the waves and thus helps in predicting the price trend.** This would become clearer from Chapter 6 on Fibonacci relationships.

Fibonacci Retracements

In the stock markets, numbers featuring in the Fibonacci sequence have generally been found to define areas of support and resistance. Those areas are identified by taking two extreme points — usually a major peak and a major trough — on a price chart and then dividing the vertical distance between them by the key Fibonacci ratios of 23.60%, 38.20%, 50%, 61.80% and 100%. Once these levels are identified, horizontal lines are drawn to indicate areas of key Fibonacci support or resistance levels from where prices may retract before resuming their move in the original direction.

Figure 4.1 illustrates how Fibonacci support levels at 23.60%, 38.20%, 50% and 61.80% are marked in both an uptrend and a downtrend.

The significance of Fibonacci sequence, the golden ratio, and Fibonacci retracements would become clearer in Chapter 5 which deals with Fibonacci relationship.

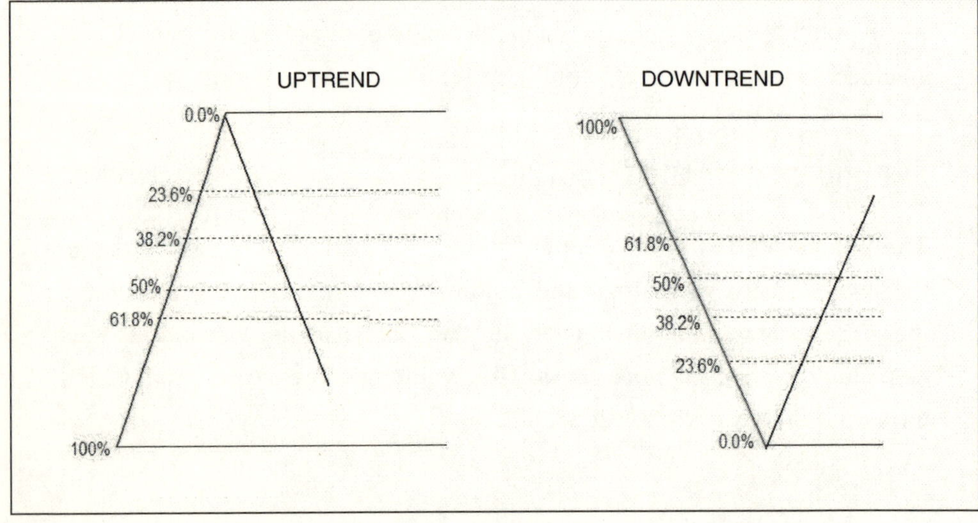

Figure 4.1: **Fibonacci retracements during up and down trends**

5

Fibonacci Relationships

Fibonacci summation series is the basis of Elliott Wave Theory since Fibonacci numbers come up repeatedly in the structure of Elliott waves. The interesting thing is that after the Elliott Wave Theory was developed, it was observed that it reflected the Fibonacci sequence.

The following Fibonacci relationships are not rigid rules but guidelines for estimating the length of the various waves.

Fibonacci Relationships for Wave 2

- Wave 2 is always related to Wave 1.
- Wave 2 equals either:

  — 50% retracement of Wave 1, or

  — 61.80% retracement of Wave 1.

Fibonacci Relationships for Wave 3

- Wave 3 is always related to Wave 1.
- Wave 3 is either:

  — 1.618 times the length of Wave 1, or

  — 2.618 times the length of Wave 1, or

  — 4.23 times the length of Wave 1.

Fibonacci Relationships for Wave 4

- Wave 4 is always related to Wave 3.
- The length of Wave 4 is either:

— 23.60% retracement of Wave 3, or

— 38.20% retracement of Wave 3

— 50% retracement of Wave 3.

- In no case is Wave 4 longer than 61.80% retracement of Wave 3.

Fibonacci Relationships for Wave 5

When Wave 3 is Longer than 1.618 Times the Length of Wave 1

- Either Wave 5 is equal to Wave 1; or
- Wave 5 is either:

— 1.618 times the length of Wave 1, or

— 2.618 times the length of Wave 1.

When Wave 3 is Shorter than 1.618 Times the Length of Wave 1

- Wave 5 is either:

— 1.618 times the entire length from the bottom of Wave 1 to the top of Wave 3; or

— 2.618 times the entire length from bottom of Wave 1 to the top of Wave 3.

Fibonacci Relationships for Wave A

- Wave A is related to Wave 5.
- The length of Wave A is either:

— 23.60% retracement of Wave 5; or

— 38.20% retracement of Wave 5.

Fibonacci Relationships for Wave B

- Wave B is related to Wave A.
- The length of Wave B is either:
  - 50% retracement of Wave A; or
  - 61.80% retracement of Wave A.

Fibonacci Relationships for Wave C

- Wave C is related to Wave A.
- The length of Wave C is either
  - 1.618 times the length of Wave A, or
  - 2.618 times the length of Wave A.

~

6

Elliott Wave Trading Strategies

The chapters that follow are the heart of this book and explain three Elliott Wave trading strategies in detail.

Rules for Trading Elliott Waves

Trading stock markets using Elliott Wave Theory is not an easy path to walk. It requires a lot of hard work and practice. I have learnt from experience that one should always follow two basic rules while trading Elliott Waves:

1. To begin with, 70% of Elliott Wave patterns are simple while 30% are complex. Hence, **the first rule is to trade those 70% of the patterns which are clearer and easier to understand**, at least to start with.

2. Corrections are difficult to trade as these are short lived. Moreover, corrective waves have potential to come to an end in a fraction of second. So, **the second rule is to always trade only in the direction of the dominant trend and impulsive waves** and not to trade in the direction of corrective waves.

Elliott Wave Trading Strategies

We'll be discussing three trading strategies at length, each illustrated with multiple real examples from the Indian markets.

1. The **first strategy** is to take a position in the direction of Wave 3, as and when Wave 3 emerges.

2. The **second strategy** is to take a position in the direction of the dominant trend as and when Wave 4 comes to an end.

3. The **third strategy** is to take a position in the direction of the dominant trend as and when Wave 5 comes to an end.

The chapters that follow are a deep dive into each of these three strategies.

7

Strategy 1: Trading in the Direction of Wave 3 When it Forms

Buying When Wave 3 Emerges in a Rising Market

Rules

- **Buy** as and when a rising Wave 3 crosses above the highs of Wave 1.
- The **stop loss** should be placed below the bottom of Wave 2 as protection against any unexpected fall in price.
- Thereafter, make use of Fibonacci relationships for predicting **Wave 3 targets**.
- **Exit** either around Wave 3 target levels as suggested by Fibonacci relationships.

  Alternately, if the stock price rise stops short of the target, or one is not able to lock profit at higher levels, then irrespective of the target one should close the buy position as and when the level of the immediate preceding fractal made during the earlier advance of Wave 3 is cracked on the down side. This signals that the rising Wave 3 might have come to an end.

Let's understand this better with real examples from the Indian stock market.

Example 7.1: Asian Paints

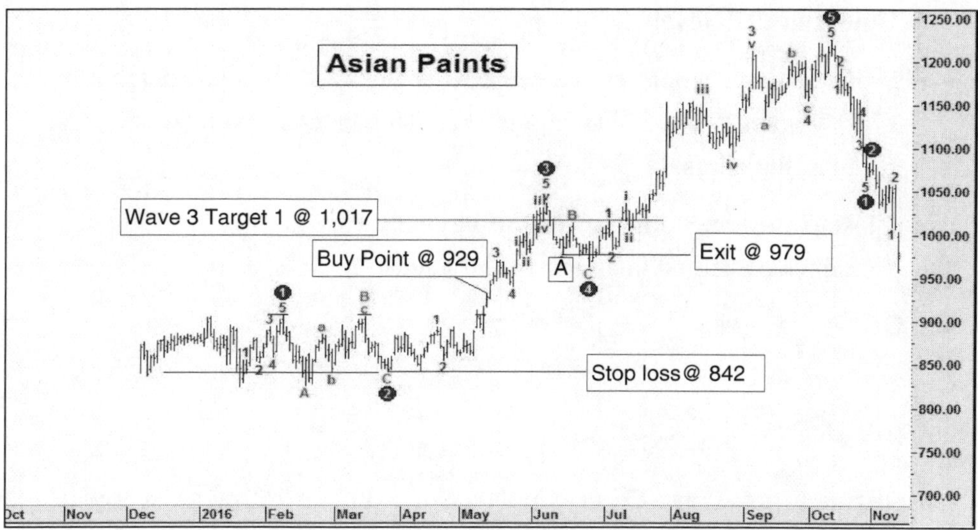

Figure 7.1: **Daily stock price chart of Asian Paints**

~

Applying Elliott Wave Theory on the chart in Figure 7.1 suggests buying as and when the stock price closes above the highs made earlier by Wave 1, i.e. buying at or around ₹929 levels. Here, the stop loss can be placed below the bottom of Wave 2, i.e. at around ₹842 levels.

The Fibonacci relationship study in this case suggests that the first price target for Wave 3 is at ₹1,017 levels, i.e. at 1.618 times the length of Wave 1.

It would have been most beneficial had one had booked profit at around ₹1,017 levels. If not, one must close the long position as and when the level of fractal [A] formed earlier by the rising Wave 3 is cracked on the downside because this signals that the rise of Wave 3 might have come to an end. Accordingly, the buy side positions must be closed at ₹979 levels.

Trade Summary

- Buying at ₹929 levels.
- Profit booking would have been best at the first price target level of ₹1,017 when Wave 3 was moving up. This would have resulted in a profit of 88 points.
- Closing the long position at the alternate exit point at ₹979 levels would have resulted in a profit of 50 points.

~

Example 7.2: BPCL

Applying Elliott Wave Theory on the chart in Figure 7.2 suggests buying as and when the stock price closes above the highs made earlier by Wave 1, i.e. buying at about ₹506 levels. Here, the stop loss is to be placed below the bottom of Wave 2, namely at around ₹445 levels.

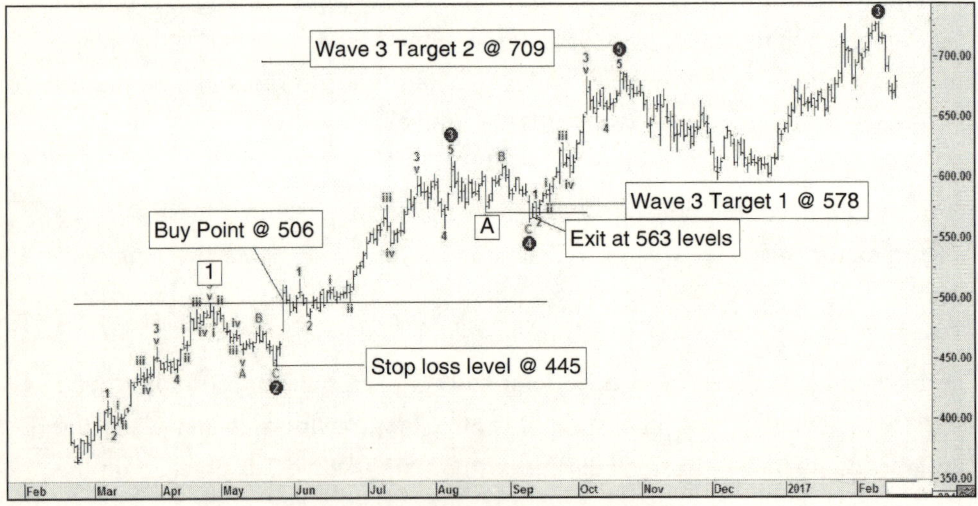

Figure 7.2: **Daily price chart of BPCL**

~

Fibonacci relationship study in this case suggests:

- The first price target for Wave 3 is ₹578 levels, i.e. at 1.618 times the length of Wave 1;
- The second price target for Wave 3 is ₹709 levels, i.e. at 2.618 times the length of Wave 1.

In the event, the stock price never rallied up to the second price target level of ₹709 during Wave 3's up move.

It would have been most beneficial had one booked profit at around ₹578 levels during the up move.

If that were not done, one must close the buy side position as and when the stock price cracks on the downside the level of the Elliott Wave fractal A (marked in Figure 7.2) formed earlier by the advancing Wave 3, i.e. closing the long positions at ₹563 levels. This is because such a break signals that the ongoing advance of Wave 3 might have come to an end.

Trade Summary

- Buying at around ₹506 levels.
- Profit booking at the first price target level of about ₹578 would have resulted in a profit of 72 points.
- Closing the buy position at the exit point, i.e. at ₹563 levels would have resulted in a profit of 57 points.

Example 7.3: HDFC Bank

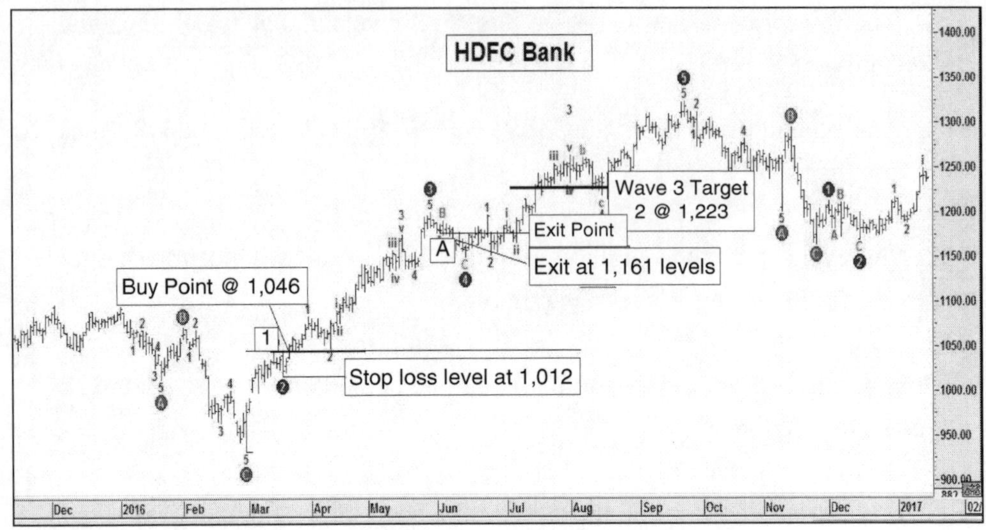

Figure 7.3: **Daily stock price chart of HDFC Bank**

~

Applying Elliott Wave Theory to the HDFC Bank chart in Figure 7.3 would suggest buying as and when the stock price closes above the highs of Wave 1, i.e. buying at around ₹1,046 levels. The stop loss is to be placed below the bottom of Wave 2, i.e. at about ₹1,012 levels.

Here, the Fibonacci relationship study suggests:

- The first price target for Wave 3 is ₹1,110 levels, i.e. at 1.618 times the length of Wave 1;
- The second price target for Wave 3 is ₹1,223 levels, i.e. at 2.618 times the length of Wave 1.

In this case, the stock price never rallied to the second price target level of around ₹1,223.

It would have been best had one booked profit at around ₹1,110 levels during Wave 3's up move. Else, one must close the buy position as and when the stock price cracks on the downside the level of fractal A formed by the earlier advance of Wave 3, at ₹1,161 levels. Such a break signals that the ongoing advance of Wave 3 might have come to an end, which necessitates closing the buy side position.

Trade Summary

- Buying at ₹1,046 levels.
- Profit booking at the first upside price target level of ₹1,110 would have resulted in a profit of 64 points.
- Closing the buy position at the exit point level of ₹1,161 would have resulted in a profit of 115 points.

~

Example 7.4: Hindalco

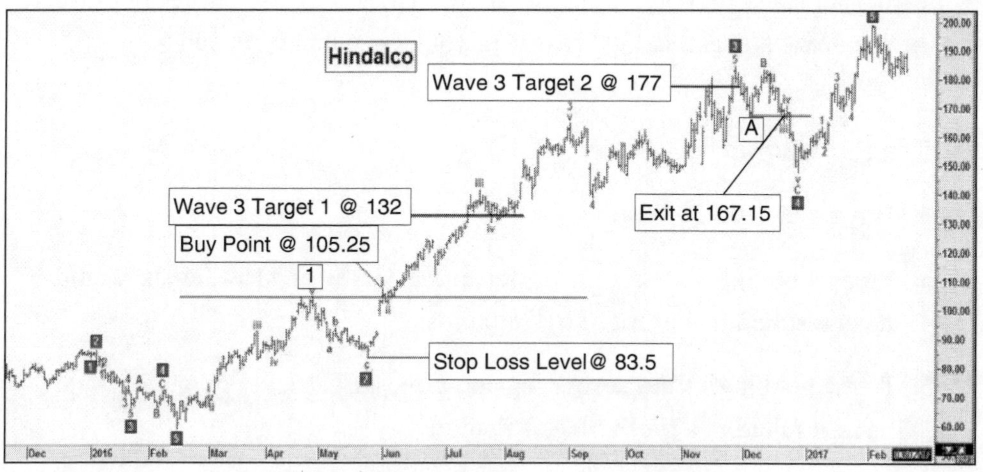

Figure 7.4: **Daily stock price chart of Hindalco**

~

Applying Elliott Wave Theory on the chart in Figure 7.4 suggests buying Hindalco as and when the stock price closes above the highs made earlier by Wave 1, i.e. buying at about ₹105.25 level. The stop loss is to be placed below the bottom of Wave 2, i.e. at about ₹83.50 levels.

In this case, the Fibonacci relationship study suggests the following:

- The first price target for Wave 3 is ₹132 levels, i.e. at 1.618 times the length of Wave 1;
- The second price target for Wave 3 is ₹177 levels, i.e. at 2.618 times the length of Wave 1.

As it turned out, Hindalco's stock price rallied to a high of around the second price target level of ₹177.

Had the trader booked profits at the higher levels, it would have been most beneficial. Else, one must close the long position as and when the stock price cracks on the downside the level of fractal A formed by the earlier advance of Wave 3, i.e. at about ₹167.15 levels. This is because such a break signal that the Wave 3 might have come to an end.

Trade Summary

- Buying at ₹105.25 levels.
- Profit booking at the first upside price target at ₹167 levels would have resulted in a profit of 61.75 points.
- Profit booking at the second upside price target level of ₹177 would have resulted in a profit of 71.75 points.
- Closing the long position at the exit point, i.e. at ₹167.15 levels, would have resulted in a profit of 61.90 points.

Example 7.5: Tata Power

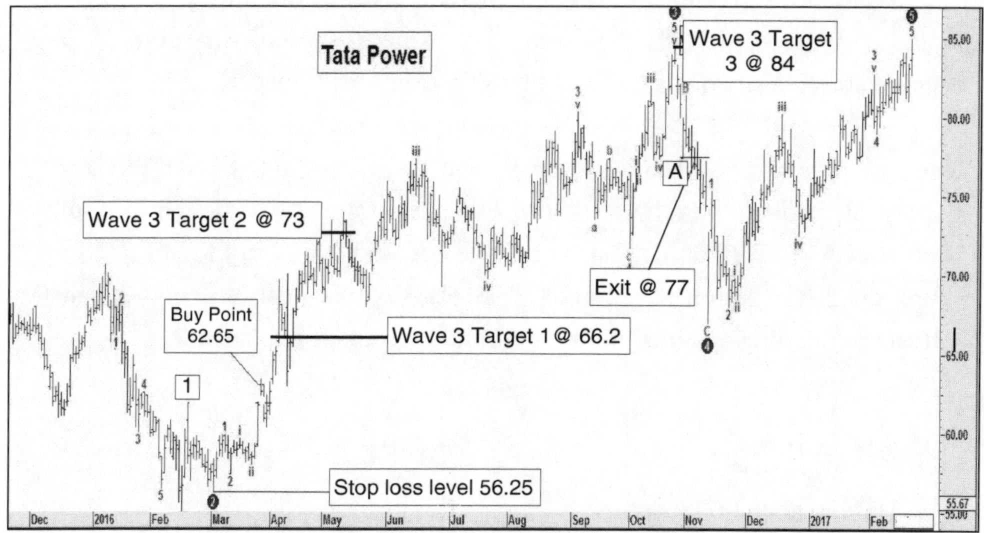

Figure 7.5: **Daily stock price chart of Tata Power**

~

Analysing Figure 7.5 using Elliott Wave Theory would suggest buying as and when the Tata Power stock price subsequently closes above the earlier highs of Wave 1, i.e. buying at about ₹62.65 levels. The stop loss should be placed below the bottom of Wave 2, i.e. around ₹56.25 levels.

In this case, the Fibonacci relationship study suggests:

- The first upside price target for Wave 3 is ₹66.20 levels, i.e. at 1.618 times the length of Wave 1.
- The second upside price target for Wave 3 is ₹73 levels, i.e. at 2.618 times the length of Wave 1;
- The third price target for Wave 3 is ₹84 levels, i.e. at 4.25 times the length of Wave 1.

Experience suggests that in such cases one must exit long positions by booking profit as soon as the rising Wave 3 reaches the third price target at 4.25 times the length of Wave 1. This is because most times the stock price corrects sharply after rallying to this third price target.

If one fails to book profit at higher levels, then one must close the buy position as and when the stock price cracks on the downside the level of fractal A formed by the earlier advance of Wave 3 — in this case, closing the buy position at around ₹77 levels, because such a break signals that the ongoing advance of Wave 3 might have come to an end.

Trade Summary

- Buying at ₹62.65 levels.
- Profit booking at the first upside price target level of ₹66.2 would have resulted in a profit of 3.55 points.
- Profit booking at the second upside price target level of ₹73 would have resulted in a profit of 10.35 points.
- Profit booking at the third upside price target level at ₹84 would have resulted in a profit of 21.35 points.
- Closing the buy side position at the exit point, i.e. at about ₹77 levels, would have resulted in a profit of 9.35 points.

Example 7.6: Tata Motors

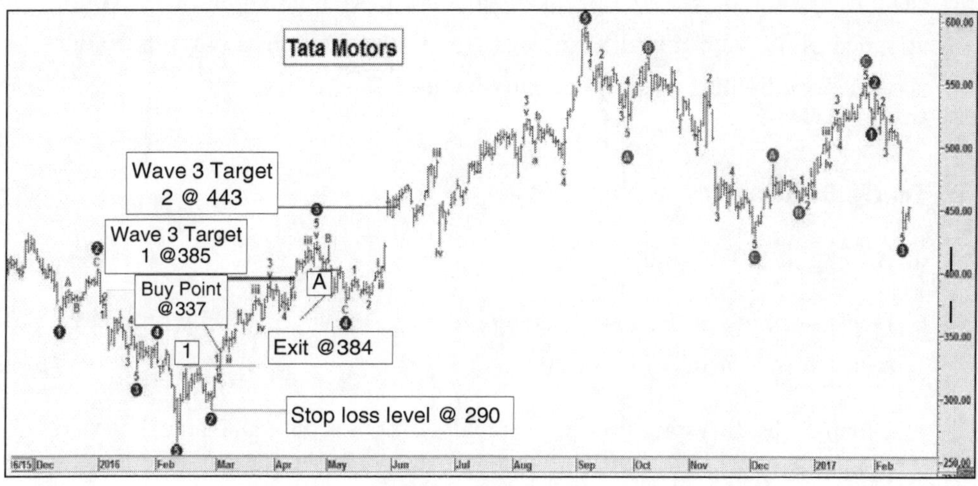

Figure 7.6: **Daily stock price chart of Tata Motors**

~

Applying Elliott Wave Theory on the chart of Tata Motors in Figure 7.6 suggests buying as and when Wave 3 closes above the highs of Wave 1, i.e. buying at about ₹337 levels in this case. The stop loss should be placed below the bottom of Wave 2, i.e. at around ₹290 levels.

Here, the Fibonacci relationship study suggests:

- The first price target for Wave 3 is ₹385 levels, i.e. at 1.618 times the length of Wave 1.
- The second price target for Wave 3 is ₹443 levels, i.e. at 2.618 times the length of Wave 1.

As it happened, the Tata Motors stock price never rallied up to the second price target during Wave 3.

It would have been beneficial had one booked profit at around ₹385 level on the upside. Else, one must close the buy side position as and when the stock price cracks on the downside the level of fractal A made by the earlier advance of Wave 3 because such a break signals that the ongoing advance of Wave 3 might have come to an end. Which is why the trader should close the buy position at ₹384 levels.

Trade Summary

- Buying at ₹337 levels.
- Profit booking at the first upside price target level of ₹385 would have resulted in a profit of 48 points.
- Closing the buy position at the exit point, i.e. at ₹384 levels would have resulted in a profit of 47 points.

~

Example 7.7: Titan

Applying Elliott Wave Theory on Figure 7.7 would suggest buying Titan as and when the stock price closes above the highs of Wave 1, i.e. buying at about ₹362 levels. In this case, the stop loss would be placed below the bottom of Wave 2, i.e. at about ₹320 levels for downside protection.

Accordingly, the Fibonacci relationship study suggests:

- The first upside price target for Wave 3 is ₹416 levels, i.e. at 1.618 times the length of Wave 1;
- The second upside price target for Wave 3 is ₹477 levels, i.e. at 2.618 times the length of Wave 1.

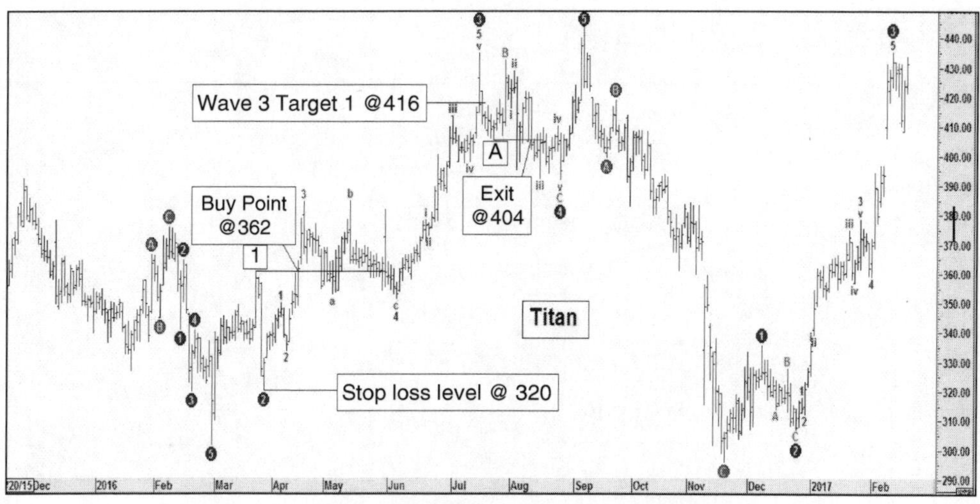

Figure 7.7: **Daily stock price chart of Titan**

~

As it happened, the stock price rallied till only around the first price target of ₹416 levels.

It would have been beneficial had one booked profit at around the ₹416 level. If not, one must close the buy position as and when the stock price cracks on the downside the level of the preceding Elliott Wave fractal A made by the earlier advance of Wave 3. Such a break signals that the ongoing advancing Wave 3 might have come to an end, i.e. one should close the buy side position at ₹404 levels.

Trade Summary

- Buy at ₹362 level.
- Profit booking at the first upside price target level of ₹416 would have resulted in a profit of 54 points.
- Closing the buy position at the exit point, i.e. at around ₹404 levels; would have resulted in a profit of 42 points.

Example 7.8: Cairn India

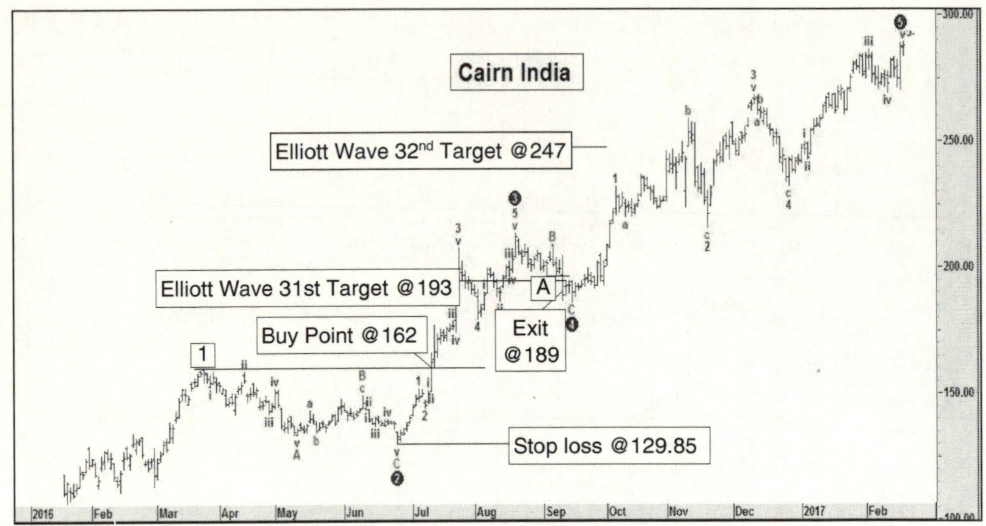

Figure 7.8: **Daily price chart of Cairn India**

~

Applying Elliott Wave Theory to the daily chart of Cairn India in Figure 7.8 suggests buying as and when the stock price subsequently closes above the highs of Wave 1, i.e. buying at around ₹162 levels. The stop loss is to be placed below the bottom of Wave 2, i.e. at ₹129.85 levels to protect against any unexpected downside.

In this case, the Fibonacci relationship study suggests the following:

- The first upside price target for Wave 3 is ₹193 levels, i.e. at 1.618 times the length of Wave 1.

- The second upside price target for Wave 3 is ₹247 levels, i.e. at 2.618 times the length of Wave 1.
- The third upside price target for Wave 3 is ₹334 levels, i.e. at 4.25 times the length of Wave 1.

As it turned out, the stock price rose only up to the first upside price target of around ₹193, and never rallied beyond to the second and third price targets.

It would have been most beneficial had one booked profit at around ₹193 levels on the upside. Else, one must close the buy position as and when the stock price cracks on the downside the level of fractal A made during the earlier advance of Wave 3. Such a break signals that the advance of Wave 3 might have come to an end, which is why closing the long positions at ₹189 levels is advisable.

Trade Summary

- Buy at ₹162 levels.
- Profit booking at the first upside price target level of ₹193 would have resulted in a profit of 31 points.
- Closing the buy side position at the exit point, i.e. at around ₹189 levels would have resulted in a profit of 27 points.

Example 7.9: Zee Entertainment

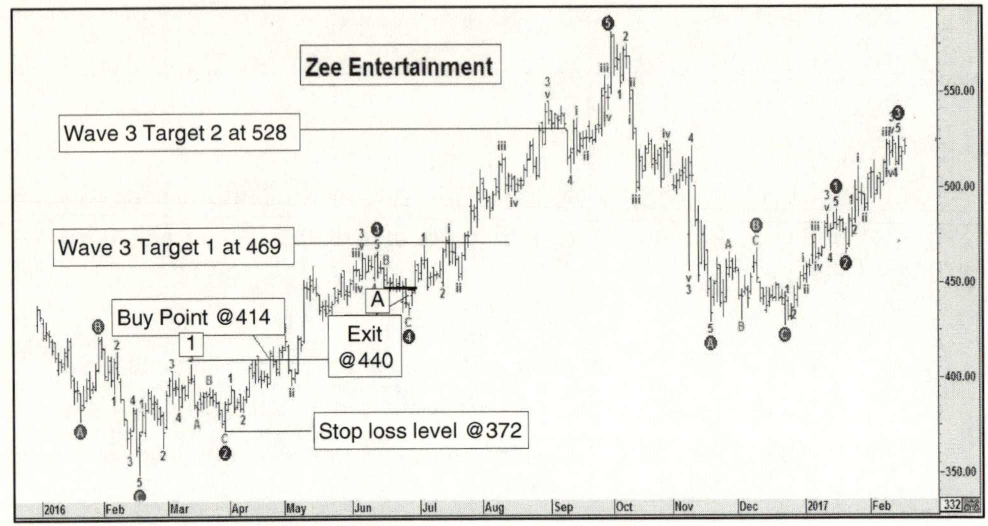

Figure 7.9: **Daily stock price chart of Zee Entertainment**

~

Applying Elliott Wave Theory to the daily chart of Zee Entertainment in Figure 7.9 suggests buying as and when the stock price closes above the highs of Wave 1, i.e. buying at around ₹414 levels. The stop loss is to be placed below the bottom of Wave 2, i.e. at ₹372 levels.

In this case, the Fibonacci relationship study suggests the following:

- The first price target for Wave 3 is ₹469 levels, i.e. at 1.618 times the length of Wave 1.
- The second price target for Wave 3 is ₹528 levels, i.e. at 2.618 times the length of Wave 1.

As it turned out, the stock price did not rise even to the first price target of ₹469. That being the case, one must then close the buy position as and when the stock price cracks on the downside the level of fractal A made during the earlier advance of Wave 3, since that's a signals that the advance of Wave 3 might have come to an end. Which is why closing the buy side positions at ₹440 levels is advisable.

Trade Summary

- Buying at ₹414 levels.
- Closing the buy position at the exit point, i.e. at ₹440 level would have resulted in a profit of 26 points.

~

Example 7.10: IndusInd Bank

Applying Elliott Wave Theory to the daily chart of IndusInd Bank in Figure 7.10 suggests buying as and when the stock price closes above the highs of Wave 1, i.e. buying at around ₹947 levels. The stop loss should

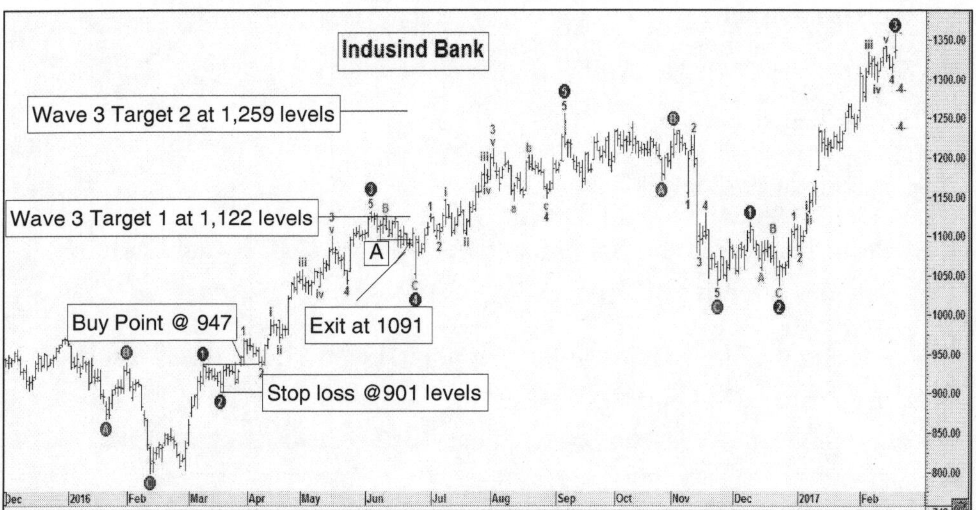

Figure 7.10: **Daily stock price chart of IndusInd Bank**

~

be placed below the bottom of Wave 2, i.e. at ₹901 levels to protect against any unexpected downside.

In this case, the Fibonacci relationship study suggests the following:

- The first upside price target for Wave 3 is ₹1,122 levels, i.e. at 1.618 times the length of Wave 1.
- The second upside price target for Wave 3 is ₹1,259 levels, i.e. at 2.618 times the length of Wave 1.

As it happened, the stock price rallied up only till the first price target of around ₹1,122.

So, one must close the buy position as and when the stock price cracks on the downside the level of fractal [A] made during the earlier advance of Wave 3. Such a break suggests that the ongoing advance of Wave 3 might have come to an end and so closing the long positions at ₹1,091 levels is advisable.

Trade Summary

- Buying at ₹947 levels.
- Profit booking at the first price target level of ₹1,122 would have resulted in a profit of 175 points.
- Closing the buy position at the exit point, i.e. at ₹1,091 levels resulted in a profit of 144 points.

Example 7.11: IndusInd Bank

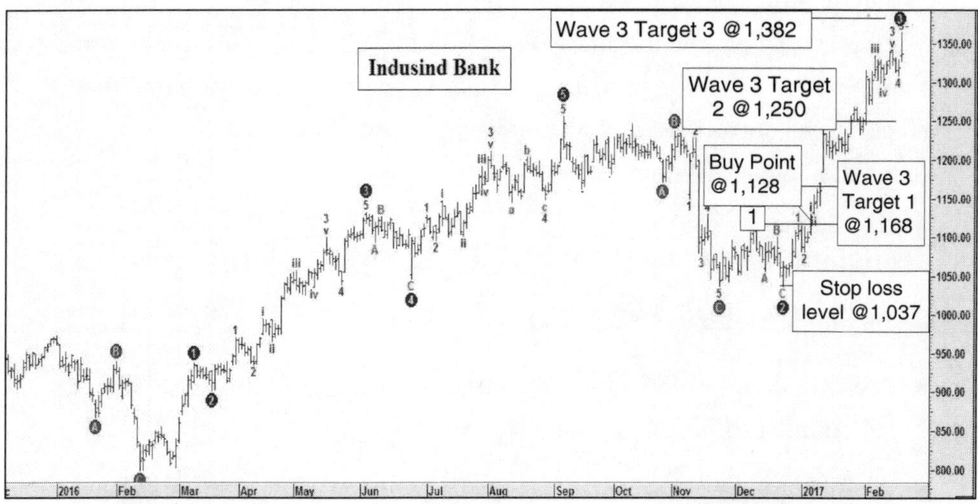

Figure 7.11: **Daily stock price chart of IndusInd Bank**

~

Applying Elliott Wave Theory to the daily chart of IndusInd Bank in Figure 7.11 suggests buying as and when the stock price closes above the highs of Wave 1, i.e. buying at around ₹1,128 levels. The stop loss is to be placed below the bottom of Wave 2, i.e. at about ₹1,037 levels to protect against any downside.

In this case, the Fibonacci relationship study suggests the following:

- The first price target for Wave 3 is ₹1,168 levels, i.e. at 1.618 times the length of Wave 1.
- The second price target for Wave 3 is ₹1,250 levels, i.e. at 2.618 times the length of Wave 1.
- The third price target for Wave 3 is ₹1,382 levels, i.e. at 4.25 times the length of Wave 1.

As it turned out, the stock price rallied upward beyond the second price target of around ₹1,250. At the time of writing, the stock's price was trading just below the third target of ₹1,382 levels. One must not hold the long position once the third price target is achieved because most times stock prices correct sharply after rallying to the third price target at 4.25 times the length of Wave 1.

Trade Summary

- Buying at ₹1,128 levels.
- Profit booking at the first price target of level ₹1,168 would have resulted in a profit of 40 points.
- Profit booking at the second price target level of ₹1,250 would have resulted in a profit of 122 points.

~

Example 7.12: Mahindra Holidays & Resorts

Applying Elliott Wave Theory to the daily chart of Mahindra Holidays & Resorts depicted in Figure 7.12 suggests buying as and when the stock price closes above the highs of Wave 1, i.e. buying at around ₹383 levels. The loss should be placed below the bottom of Wave 2, i.e. at ₹349 levels to protect against any downside.

In this case, the Fibonacci relationship study suggests the following:

- The first price target for Wave 3 is ₹428 levels, i.e. at 1.618 times the length of Wave 1.
- The second price target for Wave 3 is ₹482 levels, i.e. at 2.618 times the length of Wave 1.

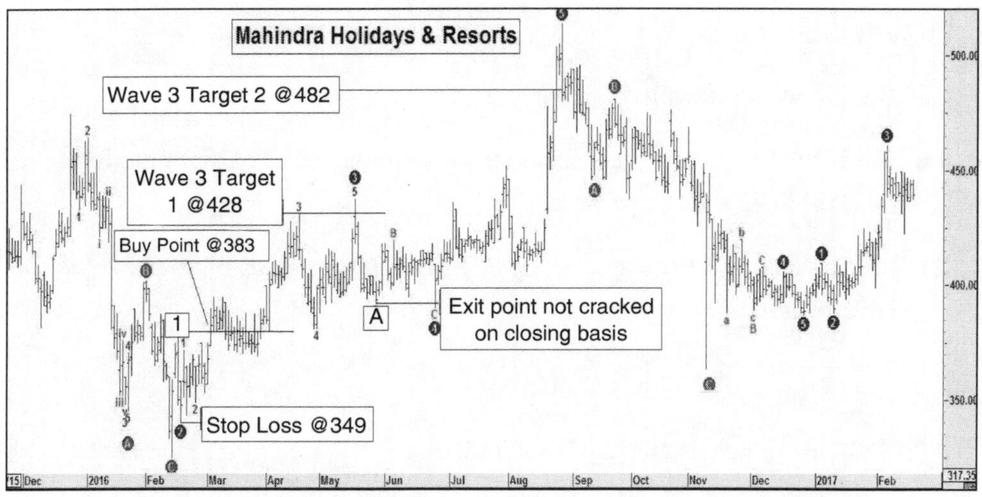

Figure 7.12: **Daily stock price chart of Mahindra Holidays & Resorts**

~

After attaining the first target levels, the stock price corrected sharply — and during this sharp correction, the wave count got altered. The buy side exit point was however not cracked on closing basis, i.e. the level of fractal A made during the earlier advance of Wave 3 was not broken on the downside. So one must continue holding the long position even if the wave count has changed.

Later, the second price target level of around ₹482, i.e. at 2.618 times the length of Wave 1, was also achieved.

I have learnt from experience that in scenarios where there is a change in the wave count, one must book profit as and when the next immediate higher target is achieved.

Trade Summary

- Buying at ₹383 levels.
- Profit booking at the first upside price target level of ₹428 would have resulted in a profit of 45 points.
- Profit booking at the second upside price target level of ₹482 would have resulted in a profit of 99 points.

~

Example 7.13: Birla Corporation

Applying Elliott Wave Theory to the daily chart of Birla Corporation in Figure 7.13 suggests buying as and when the stock price closes above the highs of Wave 1, i.e. buying at about ₹420 levels. The stop loss should be placed below the bottom of Wave 2, i.e. at ₹360 levels as protection against any downside.

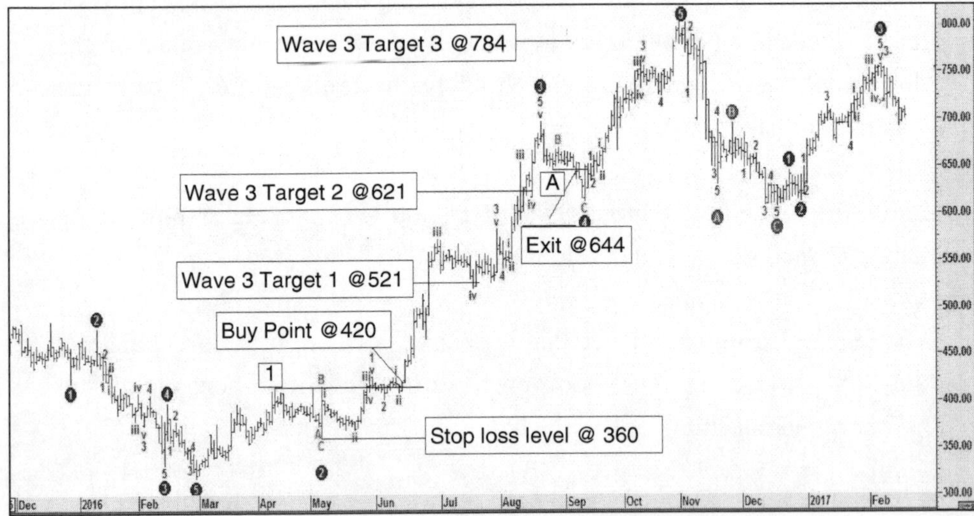

Figure 7.13: **Daily stock price chart of Birla Corporation**

~

In this case, the Fibonacci relationship study suggests the following:

- The first price target for Wave 3 is ₹521 levels, i.e. at 1.618 times the length of Wave 1;
- The second price target for Wave 3 is ₹621 levels, i.e. at 2.618 times the length of Wave 1;
- The third price target for Wave 3 is ₹784 levels, i.e. at 4.25 times the length of Wave 1.

As it turned out, the stock price rallied upward till the second price target of ₹621.

It would have been beneficial had one booked profit at higher levels. Else, one must close the buy positions as and when the stock price cracks on the downside the level of fractal A made during the earlier advance of Wave 3 because such a break signals that the rise of Wave 3 might have come to an end. So, it's advisable to close the long positions at ₹644 levels.

Trade Summary

- Buying at ₹420 levels.
- Profit booking at the first upside price target level of ₹521 would have resulted in a profit of 101 points.
- Profit booking at the second upside price target of ₹621 levels would have resulted in a profit of 201 points.
- Closing the long position at the exit point, i.e. at ₹644 levels, would have resulted in a profit of 224 points.

Example 7.14: Eicher Motors

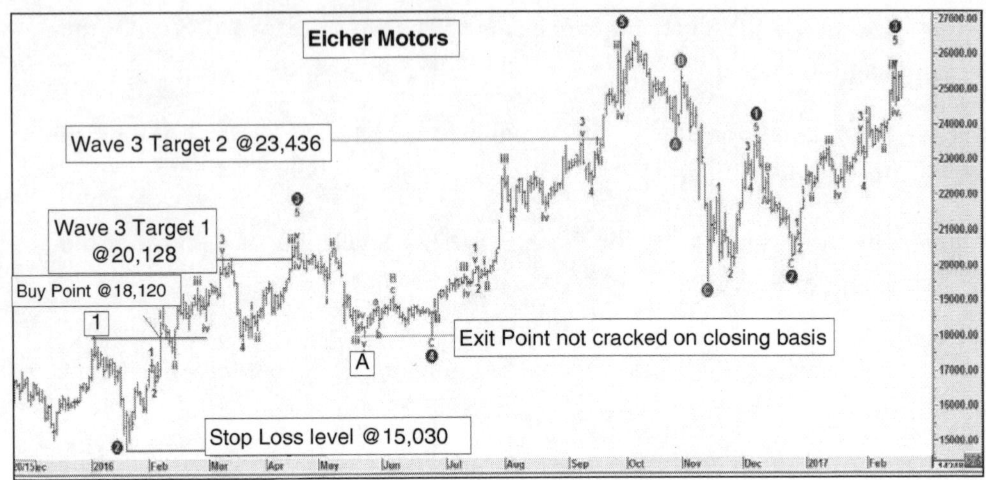

Figure 7.14: **Daily stock price chart of Eicher Motors**

~

Applying Elliott Wave theory to the daily chart of Eicher Motors depicted in Figure 7.14 would suggest buying as and when the stock price closes above the highs of Wave 1, i.e. buying at about ₹18,120 levels. The stop loss should be placed below the bottom of Wave 2, i.e. at around ₹15,030 levels.

In this case, the Fibonacci relationship study suggests the following:

- The first price target for Wave 3 is ₹20,128 levels, i.e. at 1.618 times the length of Wave 1;

- The second price target for Wave 3 is ₹23,436 levels, i.e. at 2.618 times the length of Wave 1.

After attaining the first target of around ₹20,128 levels, however, the stock price corrected sharply and during this sharp correction the wave count got altered. The exit point was, however, not cracked on closing basis, i.e. the level of fractal A made during the earlier advance of Wave 3 was not cracked on the downside. Hence one must continue holding the long position even though the wave count has changed. Later, the second price target of around ₹23,436 levels, i.e. at 2.618 times the length of Wave 1, was also attained. Experience suggests that in a scenario where there is a change in the wave count, one must book profit as and when the next immediate higher target is achieved.

Trade Summary

- Buying at ₹18,120 levels.
- Profit booking at the first upside price target level of ₹20,128 would have resulted in a profit of 2,008 points.
- Profit booking at the second upside price target level of ₹23,436 would have resulted in a profit of 5,316 points.
- Closing the buy side position at the exit point, i.e. at ₹979 levels, would have resulted in a profit of 50 points.

Example 7.15: Hero Motors

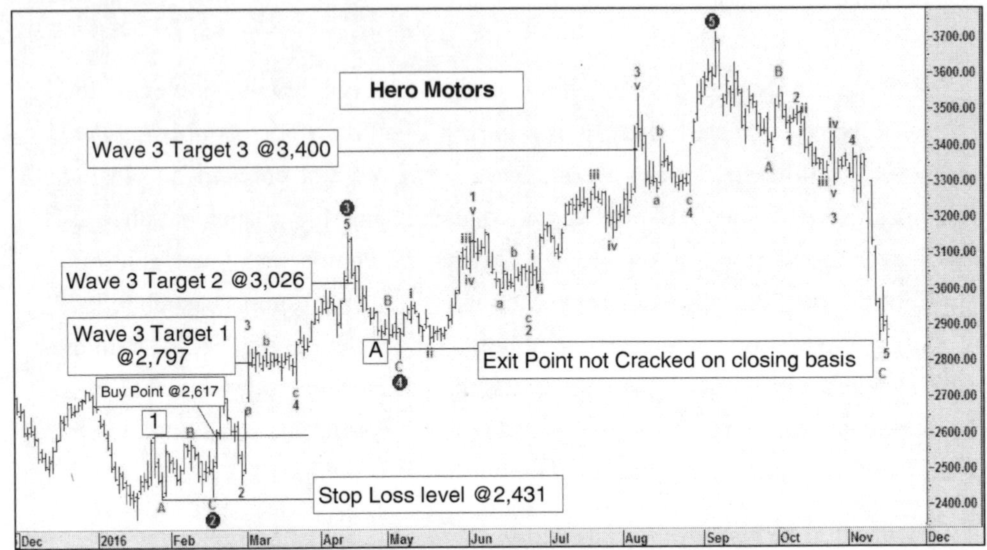

Figure 7.15: **Daily stock price chart of Hero Motors**

~

Applying Elliott Wave Theory to the daily chart of Hero Motors in Figure 7.15 would suggest buying as and when the stock price closes above the highs of Wave 1, i.e. buying at around ₹2,617 levels. The stop loss should be placed below the bottom of Wave 2, i.e. at about ₹2,431 levels.

In this case, the Fibonacci relationship study suggests the following:

- The first price target for Wave 3 is ₹2,797 levels, i.e. at 1.618 times the length of Wave 1;
- The second price target for Wave 3 is ₹3,026 levels, i.e. at 2.618 times the length of Wave 1;

- The third price target for Wave 3 is ₹3,400 levels, i.e. at 4.25 times the length of Wave 1.

As it turned out, though, the price ultimately reached the third price target, it did so after a sharp correction subsequent to its rise to the second target of around ₹3,026 levels. This correction changed the wave count but the exit point was not cracked on closing basis, i.e. the level of fractal A made during the earlier advance of Wave 3 was not cracked on the downside. Accordingly, one should have continued holding the long position even though the wave count changed.

Later, the third price target of around ₹3,400 levels, i.e. at 4.25 times the length of Wave 1, was also attained. Experience suggests that in a scenario where there is a change in the wave count, one must book profit as and when the immediate next higher target is achieved, and not wait any further.

Trade Summary

- Buying at ₹2,617 levels.
- Profit booking at the first upside price target level of ₹2,797 would have resulted in a profit of 180 points.
- Profit booking at the second upside price target level of ₹3,026 would have resulted in a profit of 409 points.
- Profit booking at the third upside price target level of ₹3,400 would have resulted in a profit of 783 points.

Example 7.16: Kotak Mahindra Bank

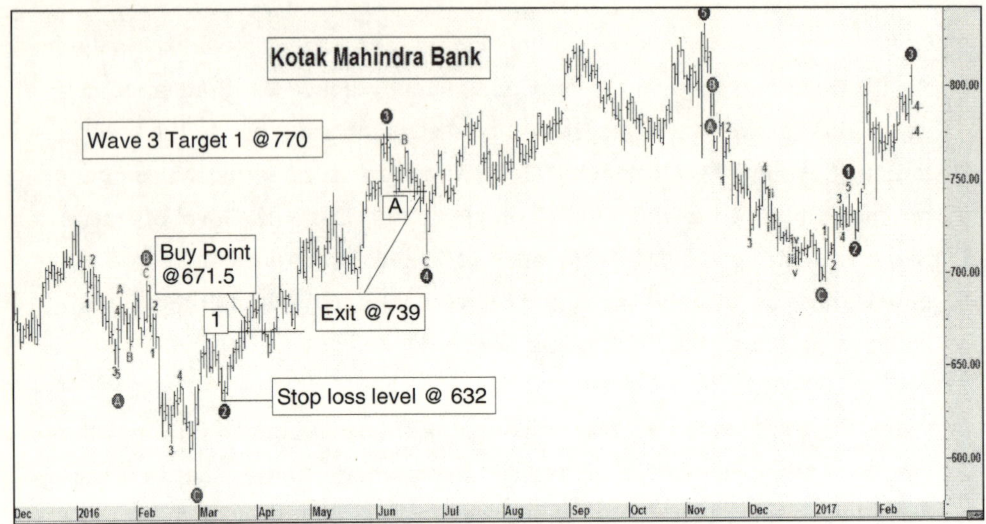

Figure 7.16: **Daily stock price chart of Kotak Mahindra Bank**

~

Applying Elliott Wave Theory to the daily chart of Kotak Mahindra Bank in Figure 7.16 would suggest buying as and when the stock price closes above the highs of Wave 1, i.e. buying at about ₹671.50 levels. The stop loss should be placed below the bottom of Wave 2, i.e. at about ₹632 levels to protect against any unexpected downside.

In this case, the Fibonacci relationship study suggests that the first price target level of Wave 3 is ₹770, i.e. at 1.618 times the length of Wave 1. Had one booked profit at around these levels, then it would have been beneficial. Else, one must close the buy position as and when the level of fractal [A] made during the earlier advance of Wave 3 is cracked on the downside. That's a signal that the advance of Wave 3 might have come to an end and so closing the buy side positions at ₹739 levels is advisable.

Trade Summary

- Buying at ₹671.50 levels.
- Profit booking at the upside price target of ₹770 levels would have resulted in a profit of 98.50 points.
- Closing the buy side position at the exit point, i.e. at about ₹739 level; would have resulted in a profit of 67.50 points.

~

Example 7.17: TCS

Applying Elliott Wave Theory to the daily chart of TCS in Figure 7.17 would suggest buying as and when the stock price closes above the highs of Wave 1, i.e. one buys at about ₹2,426 levels. The stop loss is to be placed below the bottom of Wave 2, i.e. at around ₹2,326 levels.

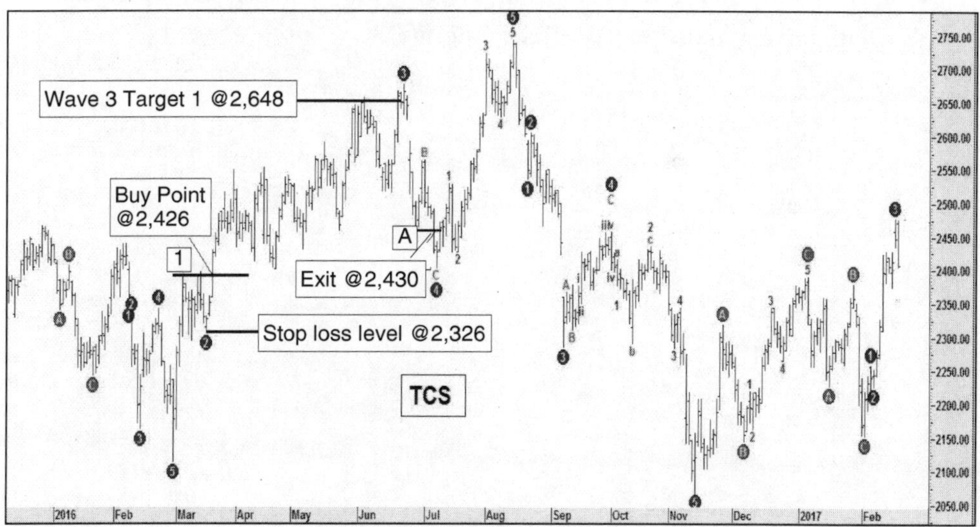

Figure 7.17: **Daily stock price chart of TCS**

~

In this case, the Fibonacci relationship study suggests a price target of ₹2,648 level for Wave 3, i.e. at 1.618 times the length of Wave 1.

It would have been beneficial had one booked profit at around ₹2,648 levels on the upside. Else, one must close the buy position as and when the level of fractal A made during the earlier advance of Wave 3 is cracked on the downside. That's a signal that the ongoing advancing Wave 3 might have come to an end, which is why closing the long positions at ₹2,430 levels is advisable.

Trade Summary

- Buying at ₹2,426 levels.
- Profit booking at the price target of ₹2,648 levels on the upside would have resulted in a profit of 222 points.
- Closing the buy side position at the exit point, i.e. at ₹2,430 levels would have resulted in a profit of 6 points.

Example 7.18: REC

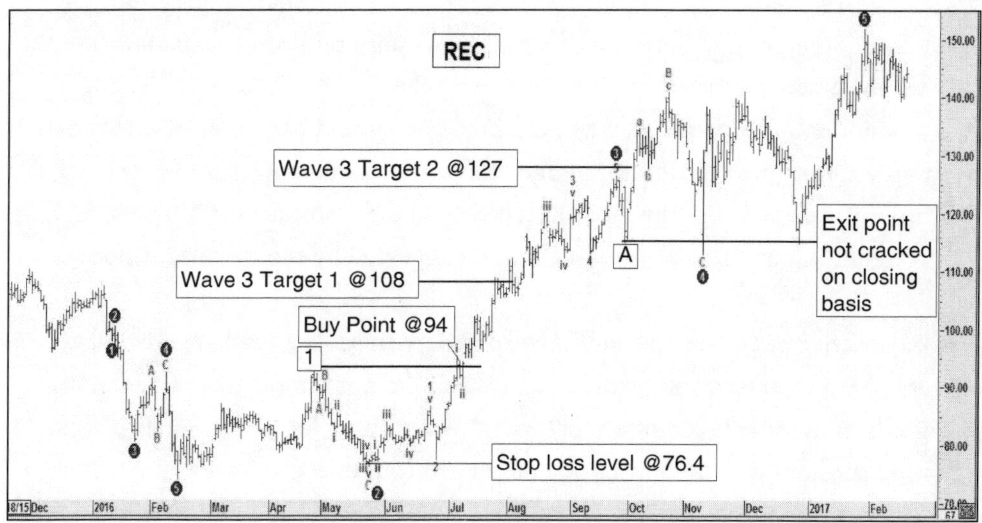

Figure 7.18: **Daily stock price chart of REC**

~

Applying Elliott Wave Theory to the daily chart of REC depicted in Figure 7.18 would suggest buying as and when the stock price closes above the highs of Wave 1, i.e. buying at around ₹94 levels. The stop loss should be placed below the bottom of Wave 2, i.e. at ₹76.40 levels to protect against any unexpected downside.

In this case, the Fibonacci relationship study suggests the following:

- The first price target for Wave 3 is ₹108 levels, i.e. at 1.618 times the length of Wave 1.
- The second price target for Wave 3 is ₹127 levels, i.e. at 2.618 times the length of Wave 1.
- The third price target for Wave 3 is ₹160 levels, i.e. at 4.25 times the length of Wave 1 (not marked on the chart as it is outside the chart's range).

In this case the stock price rallied upward to the second price target level of ₹127 — and then corrected sharply. During this sharp correction, the wave count changed but the exit point was not cracked on closing basis, i.e. the level of fractal [A] made during the earlier advance of Wave 3 was not cracked on the downside. Thus, one should have continued holding the buy position even though the wave count got changed. At the time of this writing, the stock price was trading around ₹150 levels, i.e. 10 points short of the third price target suggested by the Fibonacci study.

Experience suggests that in scenarios where there is any change of wave counts, one must book profit as and when the next immediate upside target is attained. Hence one must exit this buy position if the stock prices rally further up to the third price target of ₹160 levels.

Trade Summary

- Buying at ₹94 levels.
- Profit booking at the first upside price target level of ₹108 would have resulted in a profit of 14 points.
- Profit booking at the second upside price target level of ₹127 would have resulted in a profit of 33 points.

Example 7.19: UPL

Figure 7.19: **Daily stock price chart of UPL**

~

Applying Elliott Wave Theory to the daily chart of UPL in Figure 7.19 suggests buying as and when the stock price closes above the highs of Wave 1, i.e. buying at about ₹456 levels. Here, the stop loss can be placed below the bottom of Wave 2, i.e. at ₹420 levels.

In this case, the Fibonacci relationship study would suggest the following:

- The first price target for Wave 3 is ₹566 levels, i.e. at 1.618 times the length of Wave 1;
- The second price target for Wave 3 is ₹654 levels, i.e. at 2.618 times the length of Wave 1.

As it turned out, the stock price rose only till the first price target of ₹566. So, it would have been beneficial if one had booked profit at around ₹566 levels. Else, one must close the long position as and when the stock price cracks on the downside the level of fractal A made during the earlier advance of Wave 3 because that's a signal that the advance of Wave 3 might have come to an end. So, closing the buy positions at ₹561 levels is advisable.

Trade Summary

- Buying at ₹456 levels.
- Profit booking at the first upside price target level of ₹566 would have resulted in a profit of 110 points.
- Closing the buy position at the exit point, i.e. at ₹561 levels, would have resulted in a profit of 105 points.

~

Example 7.20: Tata Steel

Applying Elliott Wave Theory to the daily chart of Tata Steel in Figure 7.20 suggests buying as and when the stock price closes above the highs of Wave 1, i.e. buying at around ₹268 levels to protect against any downside. The stop loss should be placed below the bottom of Wave 2, i.e. at about ₹243 levels.

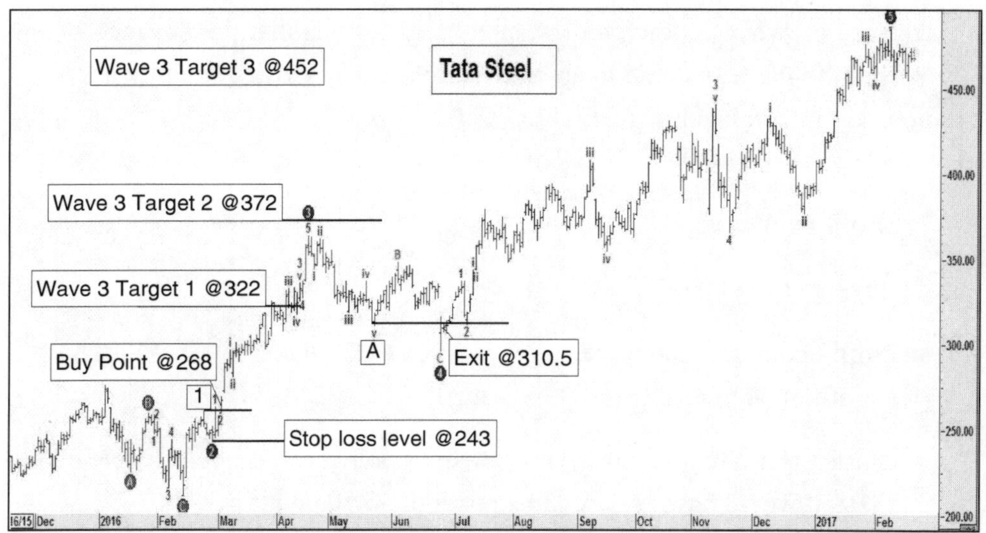

Figure 7.20: **Daily stock price chart of Tata Steel**

~

In this case, the Fibonacci relationship study would suggest the following:

- The first price target for Wave 3 is ₹322 levels, i.e. at 1.618 times the length of Wave 1.
- The second price target for Wave 3 is ₹372 levels, i.e. at 2.618 times the length of Wave 1.
- The third price target for Wave 3 is ₹452 levels, i.e. at 2.618 times the length of Wave 1.

As it happened, the stock price rallied only up to the first price target of ₹322.

Obviously, it would have been best had one booked profit at around ₹322 levels. Else, one must close the long position as and when the stock price cracks on the downside the level of fractal A made during the earlier advance of Wave 3. Such a downside break signals that the advance of Wave 3 might have come to an end. Which is why closing the buy positions at ₹310.50 levels is advisable.

Trade Summary

- Buying at ₹268 levels.
- Profit booking at the price target level of ₹322 would have resulted in a profit of 54 points.
- Closing the buy side position at the exit point, i.e. at about levels of ₹310.50 would have resulted in a profit of 42.50 points.

~

Example 7.21: IOC

Applying Elliott Wave Theory to the daily chart of IOC in Figure 7.21 suggest buying as and when the stock price closes above the highs of Wave 1, i.e. buying at about ₹220 levels. The stop loss should be placed below the bottom of Wave 2, i.e. at ₹198 levels, to protect against any possible downside.

In this case, the Fibonacci relationship study would suggest the following:

- The first price target for Wave 3 is ₹242 levels, i.e. at 1.618 times the length of Wave 1;

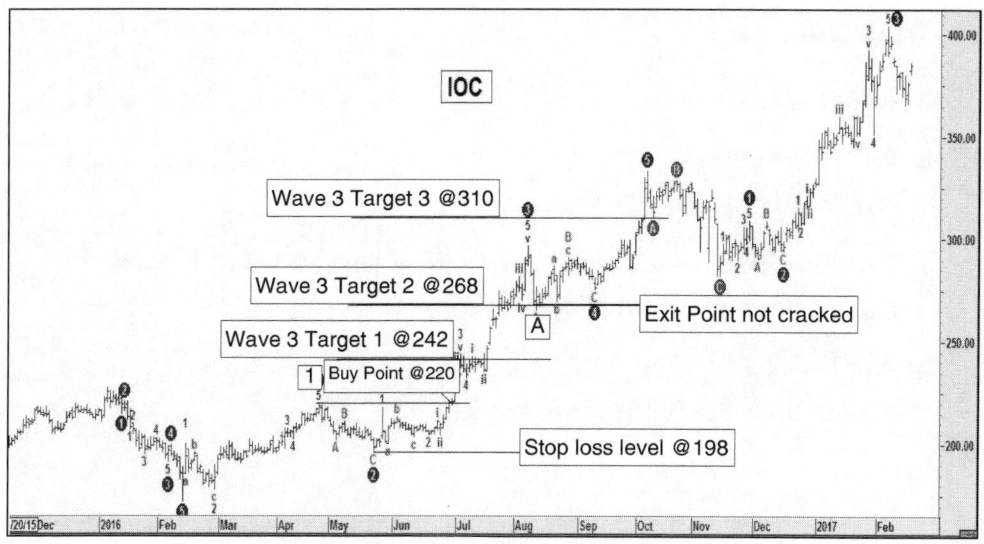

Figure 7.21: **Daily stock price chart of IOC**

~

- The second price target for Wave 3 is ₹268 levels, i.e. at 2.618 times the length of Wave 1;
- The third price target for Wave 3 is ₹310 levels, i.e. at 4.25 times the length of Wave 1.

After attaining the second upside target of ₹268 levels, the stock price corrected sharply. During this sharp correction, the earlier wave count changed but the exit point was not cracked on closing basis; i.e. the level of fractal A made during the earlier advance of Wave 3 was not cracked on the downside. Hence one must continue holding the buy position even if the wave count changed.

Later, the third price target level of around ₹310, i.e. at 4.25 times the length of Wave 1, was also attained. Experience suggests that in scenarios where there is a change in the wave count, one must book profit as and when the immediate next higher target is achieved.

Trade Summary

- Buying at ₹220 levels.
- Profit booking at the first upside price target level of ₹241 would have resulted in a profit of 21 points.
- Profit booking at the second upside price target level of ₹268 would have resulted in a profit of 48 points.
- Profit booking at the third upside price target level of ₹310 would have resulted in a profit of 90 points.

~

Example 7.22: IOC

Applying Elliott Wave Theory to the daily chart of IOC in Figure 7.22 suggests buying as and when the stock price closes above the highs of Wave 1, i.e. buying at about ₹309 levels. The stop loss can be placed below the bottom of Wave 2, i.e. at ₹289 levels, to protect against any possible downside.

In this case, the Fibonacci relationship study would suggest the following:

- The first price target for Wave 3 is ₹337 levels, i.e. at 1.618 times the length of Wave 1;
- The second price target for Wave 3 is ₹365 levels, i.e. at 2.618 times the length of wave 1;
- The third price target for Wave 3 is ₹403 levels, i.e. at 4.25 times the length of Wave 1.

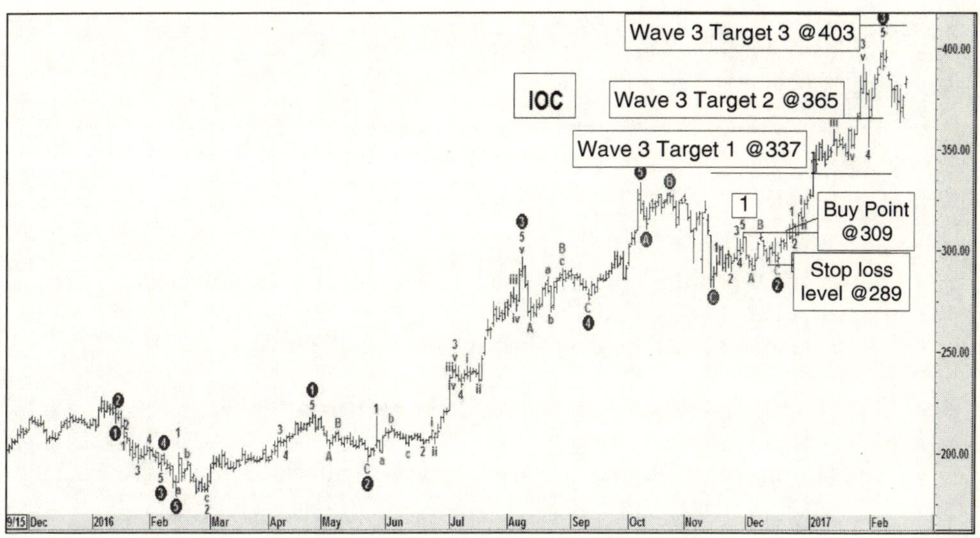

Figure 7.22: **Daily stock price chart of IOC**

~

In the event, the stock price rallied up to the second price target of ₹365. As at the time of this writing, the price was trading just below the third price target level of ₹403. Profit booking at this point would have been worth while, else one could continue holding for third price target of ₹403 levels up.

Trade Summary

- Buying at ₹309 levels.
- Profit booking at the first price target of ₹337 levels on the upside would have resulted in a profit of 28 points.
- Profit booking at the second price target of ₹365 levels on the upside would result in a profit of 56 points.

Selling When Wave 3 Emerges in a Declining Market

Rules

- **Sell** as and when the low of Wave 1 is taken off on the downside.
- The **stop loss** should be placed above the top of Wave 2.
- Use Fibonacci relationships to predict **target levels** for Wave 3.
- **Exit** around the Wave 3 target levels suggested by Fibonacci relationships.

  Alternately, if the stock price falls short of the downside target, or one is not able to lock profit at the lower level, then irrespective of the target one should close the sell position as and when the level of the immediate preceding fractal A made during the earlier decline of Wave 3 is cracked on the upside. That's a signal that the decline of Wave 3 might have come to an end.

  However, if the stock price declines to the second price target level on the downside, i.e. to 2.618 times the length of Wave 1, then one must exit the short position by taking profit straight away. That's because in most cases stock prices quickly rebound after declining to the second price target level.

Example 7.23: Tata Motors

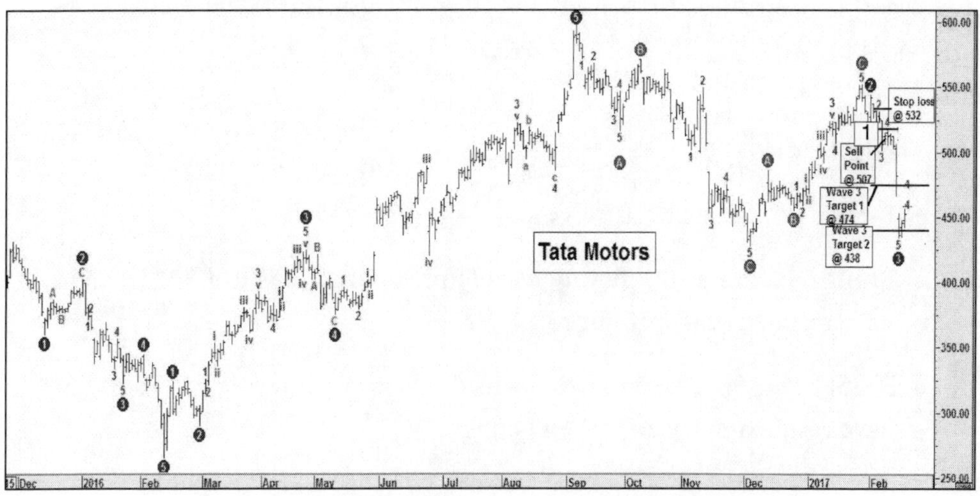

Figure 7.23: **Daily stock price chart of Tata Motors**

~

Applying Elliott Wave Theory to the daily chart of Tata Motors in Figure 7.23 suggests selling as and when the stock price closes below the lows of Wave 1, i.e. selling at around ₹507 level. The stop loss is to be placed above the top of Wave 2, i.e. at ₹532 levels, to protect against any unexpected upside move.

In this case, the Fibonacci relationship study would suggest the following:

- The first price target level for Wave 3 is ₹474, i.e. at 1.618 times the length of Wave 1;
- The second price target level for Wave 3 is ₹438, i.e. at 2.618 times the length of Wave 1.

As it turned out, the stock price declined to the second price target level of ₹438. At the time of writing, the stock price was trading around ₹452 levels.

Trade Summary

- Initiate sell trade at ₹507 levels.
- Profit booking at the first downside price target level of ₹474 would have resulted in a profit of 33 points.
- Profit booking at the second downside price target level of ₹438 would have resulted in a profit of 69 points.

~

Example 7.24: TCS

Applying Elliott Wave Theory to the daily chart of TCS in Figure 7.24 suggests selling as and when the stock price closes below the lows of Wave 1, i.e. selling at about ₹2,525 level. The stop loss should be placed above the top of Wave 2, i.e. at about ₹2,605 level as protection against any unexpected upside move.

In this case, the Fibonacci relationships suggest the following:

- The first price target level for Wave 3 is ₹2,267, i.e. at 1.618 times the length of Wave 1.
- The second price target level for Wave 3 is ₹2,057, i.e. at 2.618 times the length of Wave 1.

As it happened, the stock price failed to reach the second downside price target level of ₹2,057. Thus, it would have been beneficial had one booked profit at around the first target level of ₹2,267.

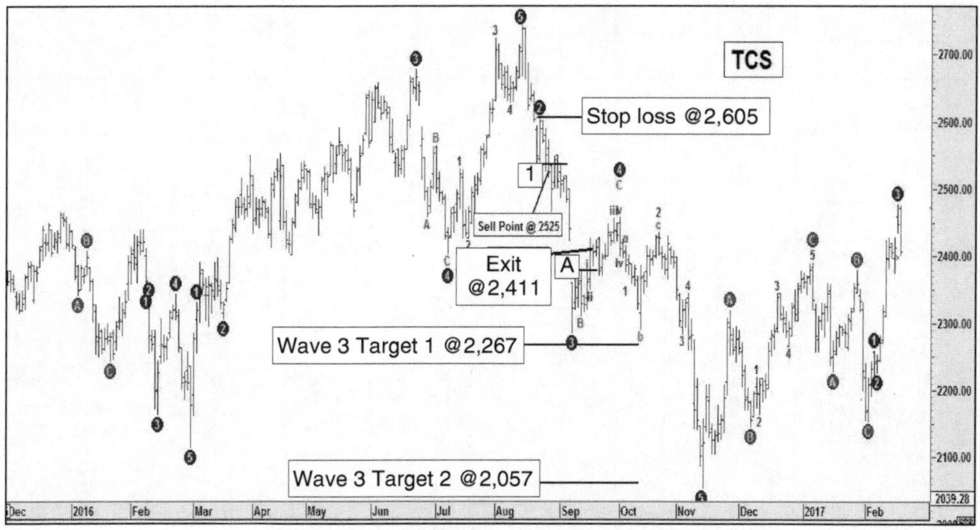

Figure 7.24: **Daily stock price chart of TCS**

~

Else, one must close the sell (short) position as and when the stock price cracks on the upside the level of the immediate preceding fractal A made during the earlier decline of Wave 3. This is because such an upside break signals that the ongoing decline of Wave 3 might have come to an end. So, it's advisable to close all sell positions at ₹2,411 levels.

Trade Summary

- Initiate sell trade at ₹2,525 levels.
- Profit booking at the first downside price target level of ₹2,267 would have resulted in a profit of 258 points.
- Closing the sell side position at the exit point, i.e. at ₹2,411 levels, would have resulted in a profit of 114 points.

Example 7.25: Arvind Ltd

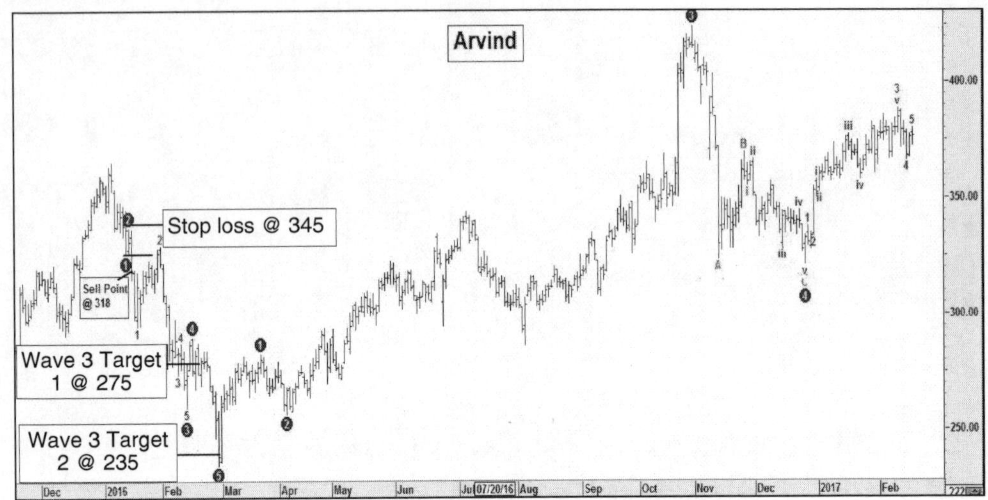

Figure 7.25: **Daily stock price chart of Arvind Ltd**

~

Applying Elliott Wave Theory to Figure 7.25 suggests selling as and when the stock price closes below the lows of Wave 1, i.e. selling at around ₹318 levels. The stop loss should be placed above the top of Wave 2, i.e. at around ₹345 levels, to guard against any unexpected upside move.

In this case, Fibonacci relationships would suggest the following:

- The first price target level for Wave 3 is ₹275, i.e. at 1.618 times the length of Wave 1;
- The second price target level for Wave 3 is ₹235, i.e. at 2.618 times the length of Wave 1.

Here, after declining to the first downside target level of around ₹275, the stock price of Arvind Ltd rallied swiftly. During this rally, the wave count changed without giving any exit signal. In such a situation, one must continue holding the short position even if the wave count has changed since the Elliott Wave study did not suggest any exit. I have learnt from experience that in a scenario where there is a change in the wave count, one must close the sell position by booking profit as and when the stock price declines to the immediate next target level. In this case, then, one must book profit at the second downside price target level of around ₹235.

Trade Summary

- Initiate sell trade at ₹318 levels.
- Profit booking at the first downside price target level of around ₹275 would have resulted in a profit of 43 points;
- Profit booking at the second downside price target of ₹235 would have resulted in a profit of 83 points.

~

Example 7.26: Aurobindo Pharma

Applying Elliott Wave Theory to the daily chart of Aurobindo Pharma in Figure 7.26 suggests selling as and when the stock price closes below the lows of Wave 1, i.e. selling at around ₹806 levels. The stop loss should be placed above the top of Wave 2, i.e. at about ₹841 levels.

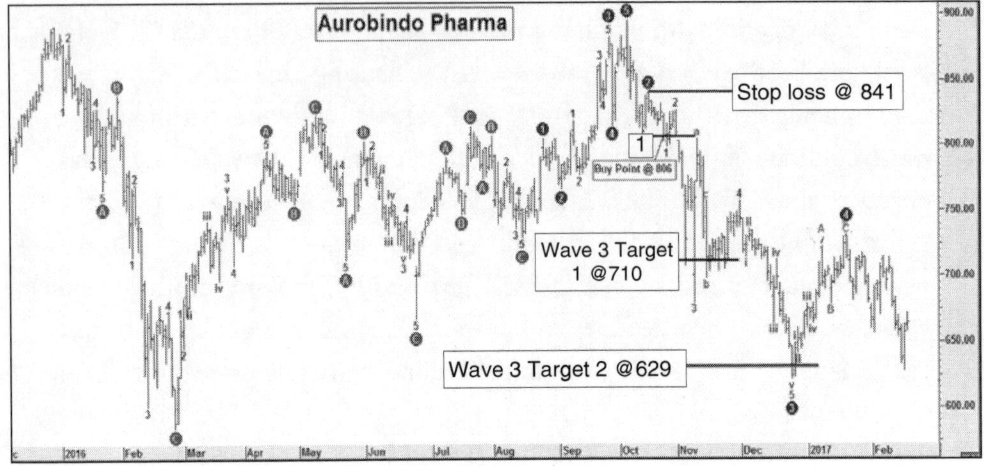

Figure 7.26: **Daily stock price chart of Aurobindo Pharma**

~

In this case, Fibonacci relationships suggest the following:

- The first price target level for Wave 3 is ₹710, i.e. at 1.618 times the length of Wave 1;
- The second price target level for Wave 3 is ₹629, i.e. at 2.618 times the length of Wave 1.

As it turned out, Aurobindo Pharma's stock price declined to the second downside price target level of ₹629.

Trade Summary

- Initiate sell trade at ₹806 levels.
- Profit booking at the first price target level of ₹710 would have resulted in a profit of 96 points.
- Profit booking at the second downside price target level of ₹629 would have resulted in a profit of 177 points.

Example 7.27: Wipro

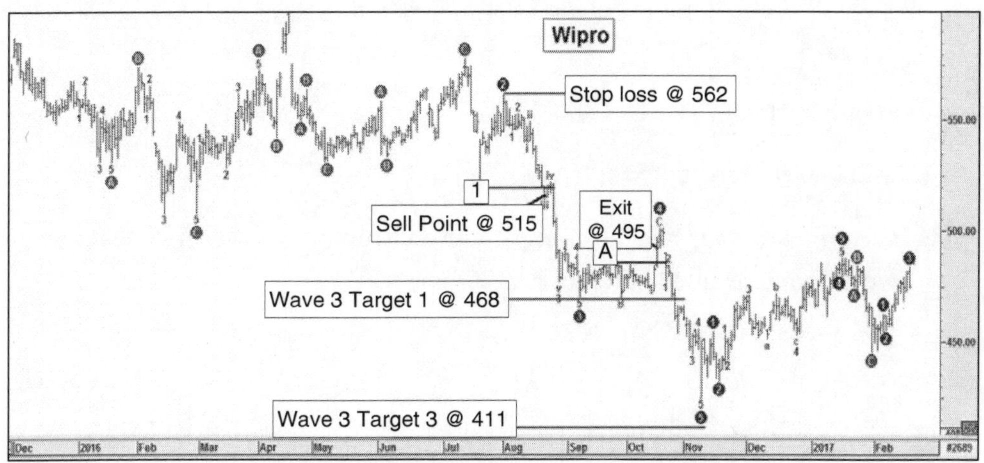

Figure 7.27: **Daily stock price chart of Wipro**

~

Applying Elliott Wave Theory to the daily chart of Wipro in Figure 7.27 suggests selling as and when the stock price closes below the lows of Wave 1, i.e. selling at around ₹515 levels. The stop loss can be placed above the top of Wave 2, i.e. at ₹562 levels, to protect against any unexpected upside move.

In this case, Fibonacci relationships would suggest the following:

- The first price target level for Wave 3 is ₹468, i.e. at 1.618 times the length of Wave 1;
- The second price target level for Wave 3 is ₹511, i.e. at 2.618 times the length of Wave 1.

Here, the stock price did not fall even to the first price target level of ₹468. So, one must close the sell side position as and when the stock price cracks on the upside the level of the immediate preceding fractal [A] made during the decline of Wave 3. Such a break signals that the decline of Wave 3 might have come to an end. So, in this case it is advisable to close one's sell position at ₹495 levels.

Trade Summary

- Initiate sell trade at ₹515 levels.
- Closing the sell side position at the exit point, i.e. at ₹495 levels, would have resulted in a profit of 20 points.

~

Example 7.28: Tech Mahindra

Applying Elliott Wave Theory on the daily chart of Tech Mahindra in Figure 7.28 suggests selling as and when the stock price closes below the lows of Wave 1, i.e. selling at around ₹485 levels. The stop loss should be placed above the top of Wave 2, i.e. at about ₹524 levels.

In this case, Fibonacci relationships would suggest the following:

- The first price target level for Wave 3 is ₹422, i.e. at 1.618 times the length of Wave 1;
- The second price target level for Wave 3 is ₹359, i.e. at 2.618 times the length of Wave 1.

The second price target level of ₹359 is not marked on the chart in Figure 7.28 as it's falling outside the chart territory.

As it turned out, the stock price declined in the beginning but thereafter rallied swiftly. During this rally, the wave count changed without giving any exit signal. Hence, one must continue holding the sell position even

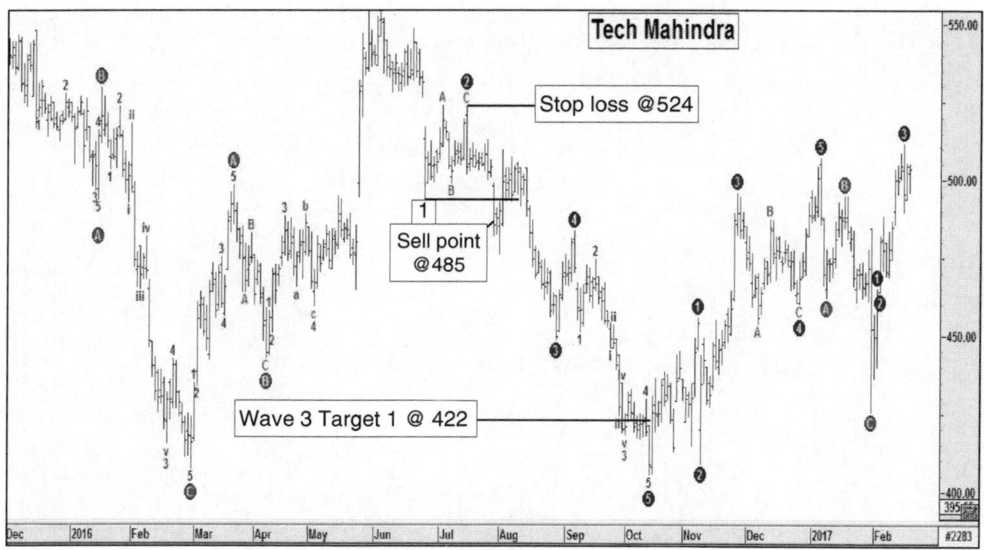

Figure 7.28: **Daily stock price chart of Tech Mahindra**

~

if the wave count has changed since the Elliott Wave study did not suggest any exit. Experience suggests that in a scenario where there is a change in the wave count, one must close the short positions by booking profit as and when stock price declines to the next immediate downside target level. In this case, then, one must book profit at the first downside price target level of around ₹422.

Trade Summary

- Initiate sell trade at ₹485 levels.
- Profit booking at the first price target level of ₹422 on the downside would have resulted in a profit of 63 points.
- Closing the sell side position at the exit point, i.e. at ₹979 levels, would have resulted in a profit of 50 points.

Example 7.29: DLF

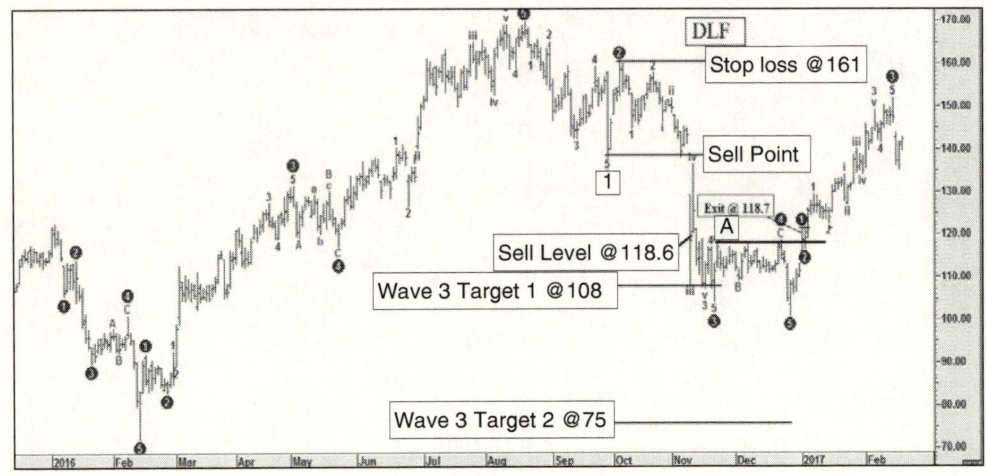

Figure 7.29: **Daily stock price chart of DLF**

~

Applying Elliott Wave Theory on the daily chart of DLF in Figure 7.29 suggests selling as and when the stock price closes below the lows of Wave 1, i.e. selling at around ₹118.60 levels. The stop loss can be placed above the top of Wave 2, i.e. at ₹161 levels to protect against any move on the upside.

In this case, Fibonacci relationships would suggest the following:

- The first price target level for Wave 3 is ₹108, i.e. at 1.618 times the length of Wave 1;
- The second price target level for Wave 3 is ₹75, i.e. at 2.618 times the length of Wave 1.

As it turned out, the stock price declined only to the first downside target price level of ₹108. Had one locked profit around this level, it would have been beneficial. Else, one must close the short position as and when the stock price cracks on the upside, the level of the immediate preceding fractal [A] made by the earlier decline of Wave 3 because such a break suggests that the decline of Wave 3 might have come to an end. Which is why it is advisable to close the sell side positions at ₹118.70 levels.

Trade Summary

- Initiate sell trade at ₹118.60 levels.
- Profit booking at the first downside price target levels of ₹108 would have resulted in a profit of 10.60 points.
- Closing the sell side position at the exit point, i.e. at ₹118.70 levels, would have resulted in a loss of 0.10 points.

~

Example 7.30: Divis Lab

Applying Elliott Wave Theory on the daily chart of Divis Lab depicted in Figure 7.30 suggests selling as and when the stock price closes below the lows of Wave 1, i.e. selling at around ₹1,161 levels. The stop loss is to be placed above the top of Wave 2, i.e. at ₹1,304 levels, to protect against any unexpected move on the upside.

In this case, Fibonacci relationships would suggest the following:

- The first price target level for Wave 3 is ₹1,067, i.e. at 1.618 times the length of Wave 1;

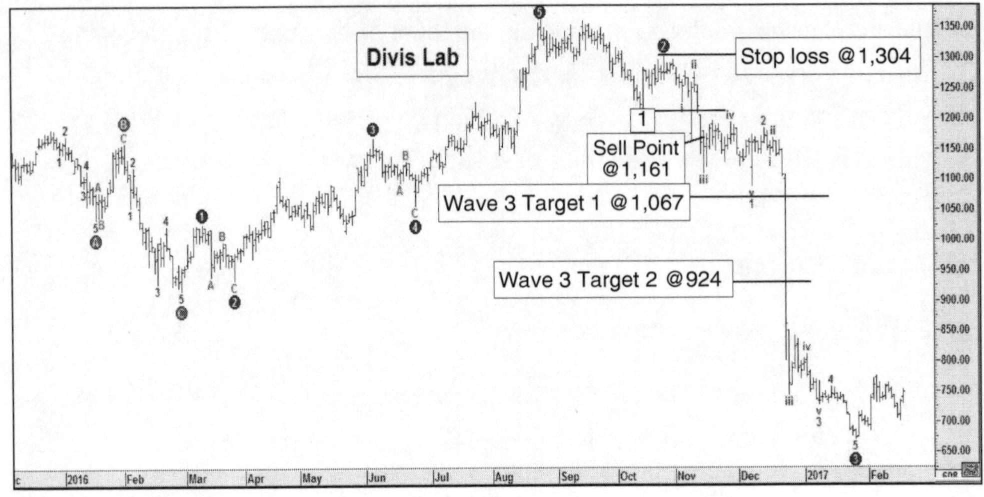

Figure 7.30: **Daily stock price chart of Divis Lab**

~

- The second price target level for Wave 3 is ₹924, i.e. at 2.618 times the length of Wave 1.

As it turned out, the stock price reached the second downside price target level of ₹924.

Trade Summary

- Initiate sell trade at ₹1,161 levels.
- Profit booking at the first downside price target level of ₹1,067 would have resulted in a profit of 94 points.
- Profit booking at the second downside price target level of ₹924 would have resulted in a profit of 237 points.

Example 7.31: HDIL

Figure 7.31: **Daily stock price chart of HDIL**

~

Applying Elliott Wave Theory on the daily chart of HDIL in Figure 7.31 suggests selling as and when the stock price closes below the lows of Wave 1, i.e. selling at around ₹83.50 levels. The sell side stop loss should be placed above the top of Wave 2, i.e. at about ₹102 levels, as protection against any price move on the upside.

In this case, Fibonacci relationships would suggest the following:

- The first price target level for Wave 3 is ₹77, i.e. at 1.618 times the length of Wave 1;
- The second price target level for Wave 3 is ₹61, i.e. at 2.618 times the length of Wave 1.

As it turned out, the stock price declined to the second downside price target level of ₹61.

Trade Summary

- Initiate sell trade at ₹83.50 levels.
- Profit booking at the first downside price target level of ₹77 would have resulted in a profit of 6.50 points.
- Profit booking at the second downside price target of ₹61 level would have resulted in a profit of 22.50 points.

~

Example 7.32: Akzo Nobel

Applying Elliott Wave Theory on the daily chart of Akzo Nobel depicted in Figure 7.32 suggests selling as and when the stock price closes below the lows of Wave 1, i.e. selling at around ₹1,561 levels. The stop loss is to be placed above the top of Wave 2, i.e. at around ₹1,724 levels, as protection against any unexpected price move on the upside.

In this case, Fibonacci relationships would suggest the following:

- The first price target level for Wave 3 is ₹1,483, i.e. at 1.618 times the length of Wave 1;
- The second price target level for Wave 3 is ₹1,333, i.e. at 2.618 times the length of Wave 1.

As it turned out, the falling stock price rallied sharply after falling till just above the second price target level of ₹1,333. During this sharp rally, the wave count changed without giving any exit signal. In such a situation, one must continue holding the short position, even though the wave count has changed, because Elliott Wave Theory did not suggest any exit. Experience shows that in such a scenario where there is change in a

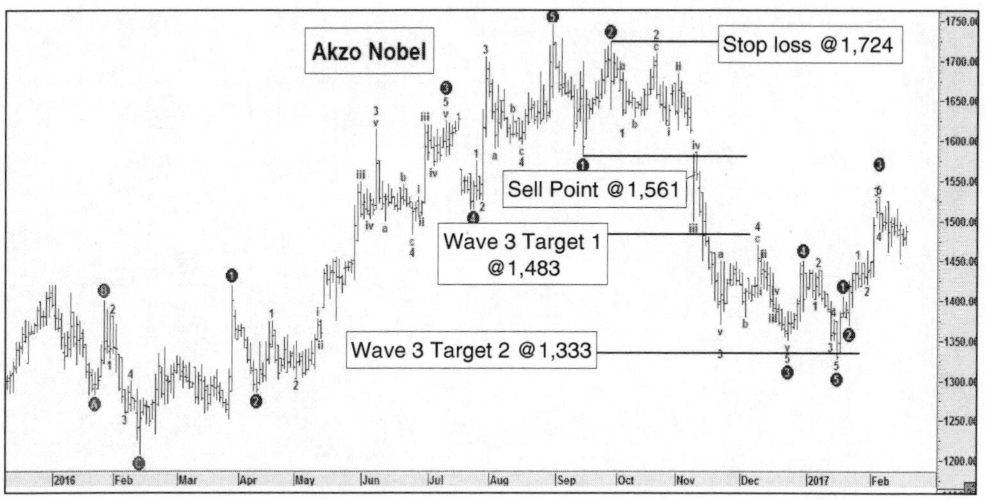

Figure 7.32: **Daily stock price chart of Akzo Nobel**

~

wave count, one must close the sell side position by booking profit only as and when the stock price declines to the immediate next downside target level. In other words, in this case one must book profit at the second price target level of around ₹1,333 on the downside.

Trade Summary

- Initiate sell trade at ₹1,561 levels.
- Profit booking at the first downside price target level of ₹1,483 would have resulted in a profit of 78 points.
- Profit booking at the second downside price target level of ₹133 would have resulted in a profit of 228 points.

Example 7.33: Bombay Burmah

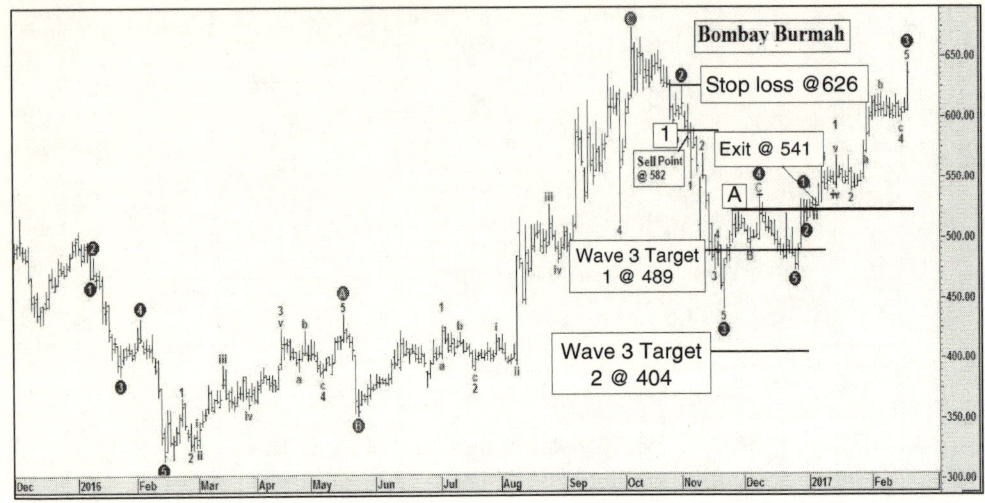

Figure 7.33: **Daily stock price chart of Bombay Burmah**

~

Applying Elliott Wave Theory on the daily chart of Bombay Burmah depicted in Figure 7.33 suggests selling as and when the stock price closes below the lows of Wave 1, i.e. selling at around ₹582 levels. The stop loss should be placed above the top of Wave 2, i.e. at around ₹626 levels.

Here, Fibonacci relationships would suggest the following:

- The first price target level for Wave 3 is ₹489, i.e. at 1.618 times the length of Wave 1;
- The second price target level for Wave 3 is ₹404, i.e. at 2.618 times the length of Wave 1.

The stock price actually declined only till the first downside price target level of ₹489. It would have been best had one locked in profits around the ₹489 levels. Else, one must close the sell position as and when the stock price cracks on the upside the level of the immediate preceding fractal [A] made during the earlier decline of Wave 3. This break signals that the decline of Wave 3 might have come to an end, so it's advisable to close the sell side positions at ₹541 levels.

Trade Summary

- Initiate sell trade at ₹582 levels.
- Profit booking at the first price target of around ₹489 levels on the downside would have resulted in a profit of 93 points.
- Closing the sell side position at the exit point, i.e. at ₹541 levels, would have resulted in a profit of 41 points.

~

Example 7.34: Brooks Lab

Applying Elliott Wave Theory to the daily chart of Brooks Lab in Figure 7.34 suggests selling as and when the stock price closes below the lows of Wave 1, i.e. selling at around ₹156 levels. The stop loss can be placed above the top of Wave 2, i.e. at ₹179 levels; as protection against any unexpected up move.

In this case, Fibonacci relationships would suggest the following:

- The first price target level for Wave 3 is ₹125, i.e. at 1.618 times the length of Wave 1;
- The second price target level for Wave 3 is ₹93, i.e. at 2.618 times the length of Wave 1.

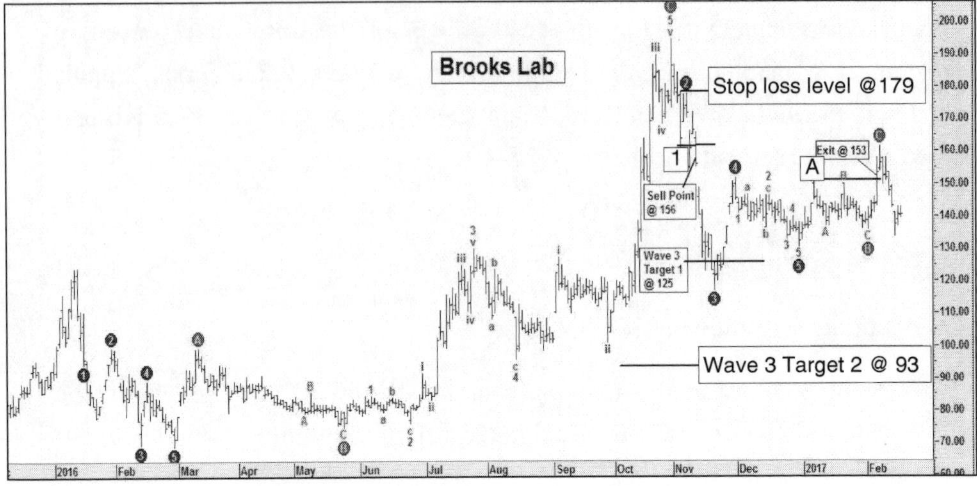

Figure 7.34: **Daily stock price chart of Brooks Lab**

~

As it happened, the stock price declined only till the second downside price target price level of ₹125. It would have been most beneficial had one locked in profit around ₹125 levels on the downside. Else, one must close the sell position as and when the stock price cracks on the upside the level of the immediate preceding fractal A made during the earlier decline of Wave 3. This signals that the decline of Wave 3 might have come to an end, so it's advisable to close sell positions at ₹153 levels.

Trade Summary

- Initiate sell trade at ₹156 levels.
- Profit booking at the first downside price target level of ₹125 would have resulted in a profit of 31 points.
- Closing the sell side position at the exit point, i.e. at ₹153 levels, would have resulted in a profit of 3 points.

Example 7.35: Apollo Tyre

Figure 7.35: **Daily stock price chart of Apollo Tyres**

~

Applying Elliott Wave Theory to the daily chart of Apollo Tyres in Figure 7.35 suggests selling as and when the stock price closes below the lows of Wave 1, i.e. selling at around ₹199 levels. The stop loss is can be placed above the top of Wave 2, i.e. at ₹216 levels to protect against any unexpected up move.

In this case, Fibonacci relationships would suggest the following:

- The first price target level for Wave 3 is ₹168, i.e. at 1.618 times the length of Wave 1;
- The second price target level for Wave 3 is ₹139, i.e. at 2.618 times the length of Wave 1.

As it turned out, the stock price failed to decline to even the first downside price target level of ₹168. So, one must now close the sell position as and when the stock price cracks on the upside the level of the immediate preceding fractal A made during the earlier decline of Wave 3 because such a break signals that the decline of Wave 3 might have come to an end, and so it is advisable closing the sell position at ₹194 levels.

Trade Summary

- Initiate sell trade at ₹199 levels;
- Closing the sell side position at the exit point, i.e. at ₹194 levels would have resulted in a profit of 5 points.

~

Example 7.36: Tree House Education

Applying Elliott Wave Theory to the daily chart of Tree House Education in Figure 7.36 suggests selling as and when the stock price closes below the lows of Wave 1, i.e. selling at around ₹168 level. The stop loss can be placed above the top of Wave 2, i.e. at about ₹198 levels.

In this case, Fibonacci relationships would suggest the following:

- The first price target level for Wave 3 is ₹93, i.e. at 1.618 times the length of Wave 1;
- The second price target level for Wave 3 is ₹19, i.e. at 2.618 times the length of Wave 1.

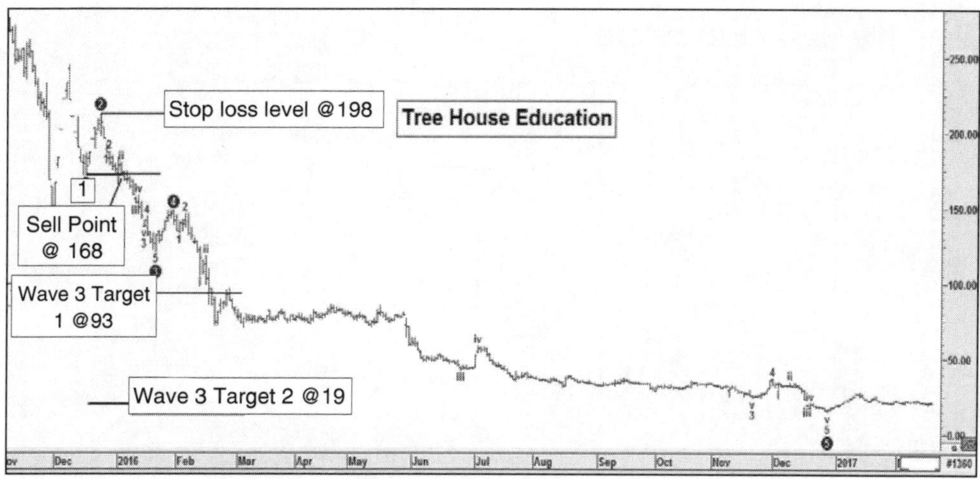

Figure 7.36: **Daily stock price chart of Tree House Education**

~

When the stock price was some distance above the first target price level of ₹93, it rose sharply, and during this rally the wave count changed without giving any exit signal. In such a situation, one must continue holding the position since the Elliott Wave study did not suggest any exit. I have learnt from experience that in scenarios where there is a change in the wave count, one must close the sell position and book profit only as and when the stock price declines to the immediate next downside target level. In other words, here one must book profit at the first price target level of around ₹93.

Trade Summary

- Initiate sell trade at ₹169 levels.
- Profit booking at the first downside price target at ₹93 levels would have resulted in a profit of 76 points.

Example 7.37: Hexaware

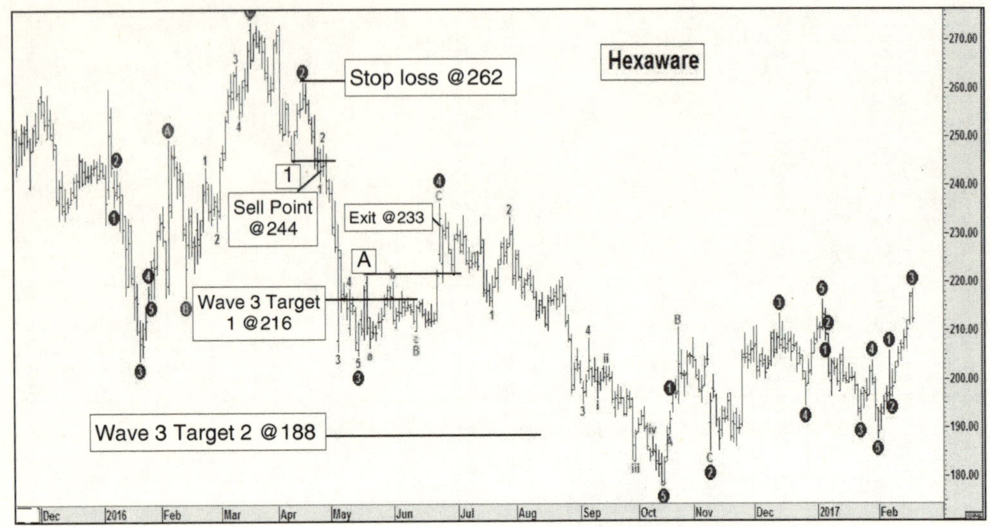

Figure 7.37: **Daily stock price chart of Hexaware**

~

Applying Elliott Wave Theory to the daily chart of Hexaware in Figure 7.37 suggests selling as and when the stock price closes below the lows of Wave 1, i.e. selling at around ₹244 levels. The stop loss is to be placed above the top of Wave 2, i.e. at ₹262 levels.

In this case, Fibonacci relationships would suggest the following:

- The first price target level for Wave 3 is ₹216, i.e. at 1.618 times the length of Wave 1;
- The second price target level for Wave 3 is ₹188, i.e. at 2.618 times the length of Wave 1.

As it turned out, the stock price declined only till the second target level of ₹216. Had one locked in profit around the ₹216 level, then it would have been most beneficial. Else, one must close the sell position as and when the stock price cracks on the upside the immediate preceding fractal [A] made during the earlier decline of Wave 3. Such a break signals that the decline of Wave 3 might have come to an end, so it's advisable to close all short positions at ₹233 levels.

Trade Summary

- Initiate sell trade at ₹244 levels.
- Profit booking at the first downside price target level of ₹216 would have resulted in a profit of 28 points.
- Closing the sell position at the exit point, i.e. at ₹233 levels, would have resulted in a profit of 11 points.

~

Example 7.38: KPIT Technology

Applying Elliott Wave Theory on the chart of KPIT Technology in Figure 7.38 would suggest selling as and when the stock price closes below the lows of Wave 1, i.e. selling at about ₹157 levels. The stop loss should be placed above the top of Wave 2, i.e. at about ₹187 levels.

Accordingly, Fibonacci relationships would suggest:

- The first price target level for Wave 3 is ₹151, i.e. at 1.618 times the length of Wave 1;

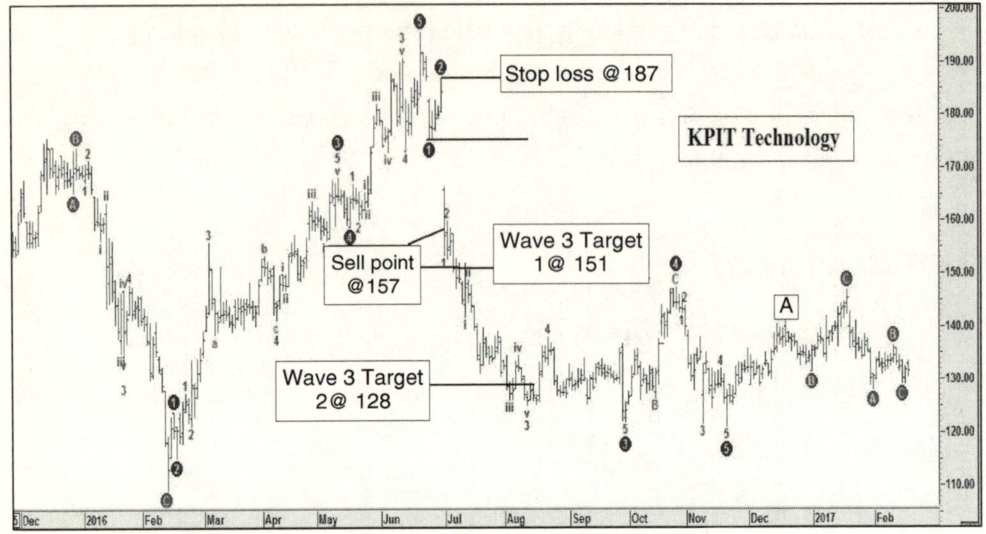

Figure 7.38: **Daily stock price chart of KPIT Technology**

~

- The second price target level for Wave 3 is ₹128, i.e. at 2.618 times the length of Wave 1.

As it turned out, the stock price of KPIT Technology declined to the second price target level of ₹128.

Trade Summary

- Initiate sell trade at ₹157 levels.
- Profit booking at the first downside price target level of ₹151 level would have resulted in a profit of 7 points.
- Profit booking at the second downside price target level of ₹128 would have resulted in a profit of 29 points.

Example 7.39: Intellect Design Arena

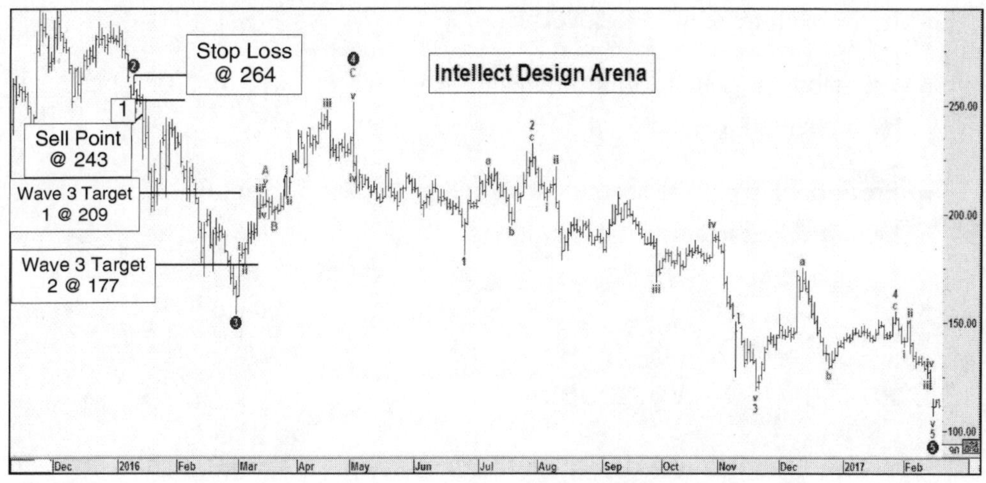

Figure 7.39: **Daily stock price chart of Intellect Design Arena**

~

Applying Elliott Wave Theory to the daily chart of Intellect Design Arena in Figure 7.39 suggests selling as and when the stock price closes below the lows of Wave 1, i.e. selling at around ₹243 levels. The stop loss is to be placed above the top of Wave 2, i.e. at ₹264 levels.

In this case, Fibonacci relationships would suggest the following:

- The first price target level for Wave 3 is ₹209, i.e. at 1.618 times the length of Wave 1;
- The second price target level for Wave 3 is ₹177, i.e. at 2.618 times the length of Wave 1.

As it turned out, the stock price fell till the second price target level of ₹177.

Trade Summary

- Initiate sell trade at ₹243 levels.
- Profit booking at the first downside price target level of ₹209 would have resulted in a profit of 34 points.
- Profit booking at the second downside price target level of ₹177 would have resulted in a profit of 66 points.

~

Example 7.40: Whirlpool

Applying Elliott Wave Theory on the daily chart of Whirlpool in Figure 7.40 suggests selling as and when the stock price closes below the lows of Wave 1, i.e. selling at around ₹1,100 levels. Accordingly, the stop loss can be placed above the top of Wave 2, i.e. at about ₹1,174 levels.

In this case, Fibonacci relationships would suggest the following:

- The first price target level for Wave 3 is ₹1,027, i.e. at 1.618 times the length of Wave 1;
- The second price target level for Wave 3 is ₹940, i.e. at 2.618 times the length of Wave 1.

As it turned out, the stock price declined to the second downside price target level of ₹940.

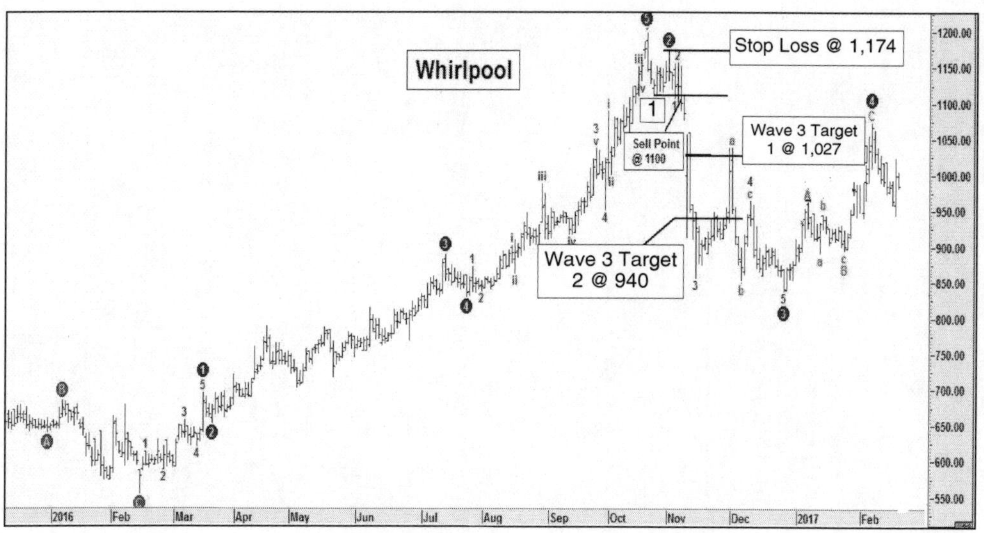

Figure 7.40: **Daily stock price chart of Whirlpool**

~

Trade Summary

- Initiate sell trade at ₹1,100 levels.
- Profit booking at the first downside price target level of ₹1,027 would have resulted in a profit of 73 points.
- Profit booking at the second downside price target level of ₹940 would have resulted in a profit of 160 points.

~

8

Strategy 2: Trading in the Direction of the Dominant Trend When Wave 4 Ends

Our second strategy involves trading in the direction of the dominant trend as and when Wave 4 comes to an end.

This strategy is further subdivided into two components:

1. Buying when the Wave 4 correction comes to an end in an advancing market;

2. Selling when the Wave 4 pullback comes to an end in a declining market.

Buying When Wave 4 Ends in an Advancing Market

Rules

- **Buy** as and when the level of the immediate preceding fractal B made during the earlier decline of Wave 4 is cracked on the upside since such a break signals that the Wave 4 correction might have come to an end. Thereafter, if Wave 4 correction was not more than 61.80% retracement of Wave 3, in most cases the advancing Wave 5 would be a strong rally. Else, the advancing Wave 5 is likely to be a weak rally and the odds of its failure increase.

- **Stop loss** for buying at the end of Wave 4 should be placed below the 61.80% retracement level of Wave 3.

- The **target** for Wave 5 is to be predicted using Fibonacci relationships.

- **Exit** should be around the Wave 5 target levels suggested by Fibonacci study unless the price falls short of the upside target, in which case you should exit the long positions as follows:

- Exit as and when the level of the immediate preceding fractal iv made during the earlier advance of Wave 5 is cracked on the downside because such a break signals that the advance of Wave 5 might have come to an end.
- Exit as and when the bottom of Wave A is cracked on the downside when the price moves down from Wave B to Wave C.
- Exit as and when the bottom of Wave 1 is cracked on the downside when the price moves down from Wave 2 to Wave 3.

Let's grasp this strategy better with the help of real examples from the Indian stock market.

~

Example 8.1: Asian Paints

Applying Elliott Wave Theory on the chart of Asian Paints in Figure 8.1 suggests buying as and when the stock price closes above the level made by the immediate preceding fractal B during the earlier decline of Wave 4, i.e. buying at around ₹1,033 levels. The stop loss can be placed below the 61.80% retracement level of Wave 3, i.e. at about ₹917 levels.

In this case, Fibonacci relationships would suggest the first upside price target level of ₹1,165 for the advancing Wave 5.

It would have been most beneficial had one booked profit around these levels. Else, one must close the buy position as and when the level of the immediate preceding fractal iv made during the earlier advance of Wave 5 is cracked on the downside. This is because such a break signals that the advance of Wave 5 has come to an end. Accordingly, the buy side positions should be closed at ₹1,091 levels.

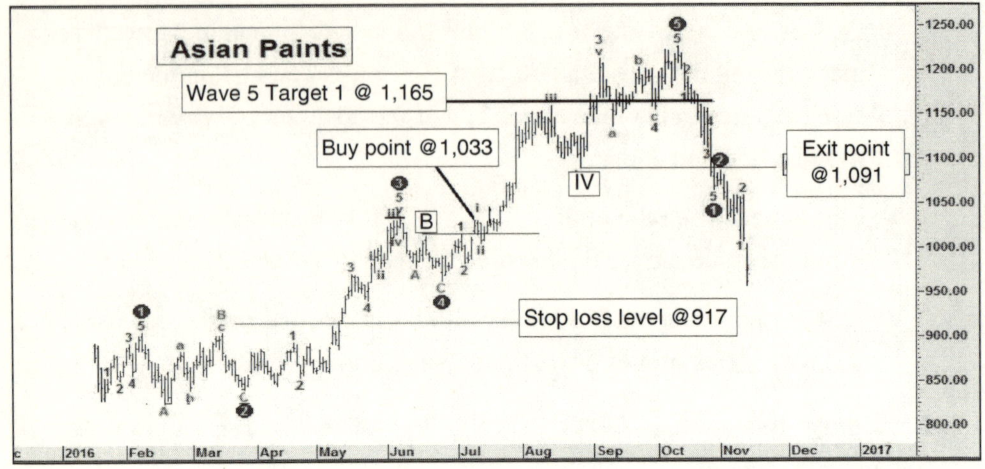

Figure 8.1: **Daily stock price chart of Asian Paints**

~

Trade Summary

- Initiate buy trade at ₹1,033 levels.
- Profit booking at the first upside price target level of ₹1,165 would have resulted in a profit of 132 points.
- Closing the buy side position at the exit point, i.e. at ₹1,091 levels, would have given a profit of 58 points.

~

Example 8.2: BPCL

Applying Elliott Wave Theory on Figure 8.2 suggests buying as and when the stock price closes above the level made by the immediate preceding fractal B during the earlier decline of Wave 4, i.e. buying at about ₹623 levels. The stop loss should be placed at or below the 61.80% retracement level of Wave 3, i.e. at about ₹510 levels, to protect against any adverse down move. In this case, Fibonacci relationships would suggest the first upside price target level of ₹691 for the advancing Wave 5.

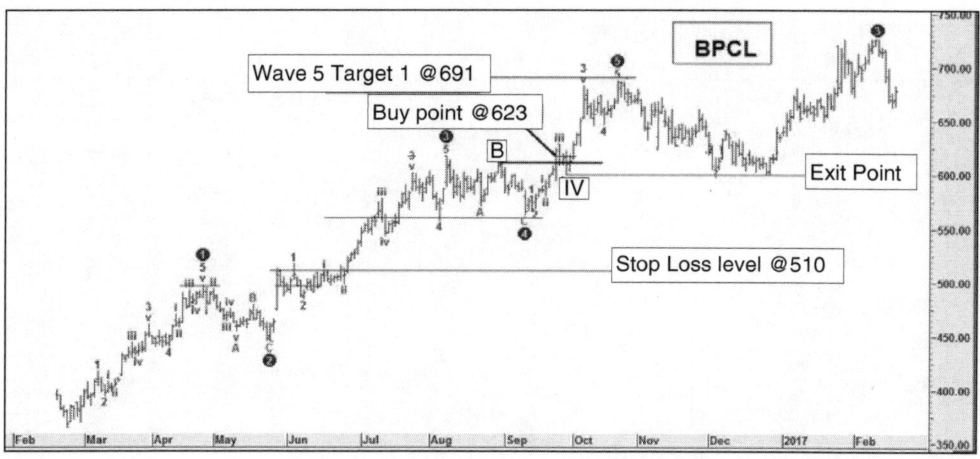

Figure 8.2: **Daily stock price chart of BPCL**

~

As it happened, the stock price entered into a correction mode after it almost reached the target level of ₹691. During this correction, the level of the immediate preceding fractal iv made by the earlier advance of Wave 5 was, however, not cracked on the downside, i.e. the price did not close below this point. Thereafter, the price started rallying again and achieved the upside target level of ₹691 on the second attempt.

Experience suggests that in a scenario where there is a change in wave count, one must close the sell positions and book profit as soon as the price rallies to the next immediate higher target level. Thus, in this case one must book profit at ₹691 levels.

Trade Summary

- Initiate buy trade at ₹623 levels.
- Profit booking at the first upside price target level at ₹691 would have resulted in a profit of 68 points.

Example 8.3: HDFC Bank

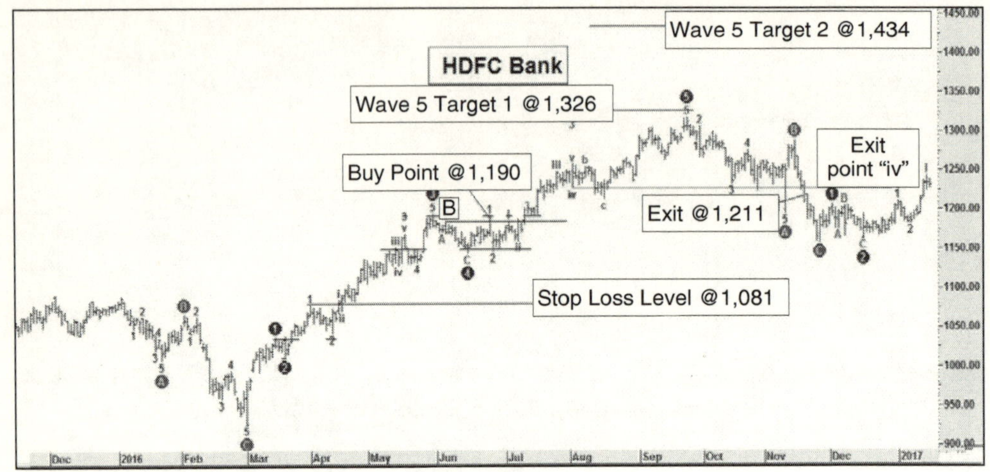

Figure 8.3: **Daily stock price chart of HDFC Bank**

~

Applying Elliott Wave Theory on the chart of HDFC Bank depicted in Figure 8.3 suggests buying as and when the stock's price closes above the level made by fractal B during the earlier decline of Wave 4, i.e. buying at around ₹1,190 levels. As protection against any unexpected downside, the stop loss would be placed at or below the 61.80% retracement level of Wave 3, i.e. at about ₹1,081 levels.

Since the length of Wave 3 is more than 1.618 times that of Wave 1, Fibonacci relationships would suggest the following:

- The first price target level for Wave 5 is ₹1,326, i.e. at 1.618 times the length of Wave 1;
- The second price target level for Wave 5 is ₹1,434, i.e. at 2.618 times the length of Wave 1.

In this case, the stock price failed to rally to even the first upside target level of ₹1,326. So one must close the buy position as and when the level made by the immediate preceding fractal iv during the earlier advance of Wave 5 is cracked on the downside. Such a break signals that the rise of Wave 5 has come to an end, and so the long position should be closed at or around ₹1,211 levels.

Trade Summary

- Initiate buy trade at ₹1,190 levels.
- Closing the buy position at the exit point, i.e. at ₹1,211 levels would have given a profit of 21 points.

~

Example 8.4: Hindalco

Applying Elliott Wave Theory on the daily chart of Hindalco in Figure 8.4 suggests buying as and when the stock price closes above the level of fractal B made during the earlier decline of Wave 4, i.e. buying at about ₹187.15 level. The stop loss should be placed at or below the 61.80% retracement level of Wave 3, i.e. at ₹121.55 levels to protect against any unexpected downside.

Since Wave 3 is more than 1.618 times the length of Wave 1, Fibonacci relationships would suggest the following:

- The first price target level for Wave 5 is ₹212, i.e. at 1.618 times the length of Wave 1;
- The second price target level for Wave 5 is ₹258, i.e. at 2.618 times the length of Wave 1.

These target levels are not marked in Figure 8.4 as they fall outside this chart's territory.

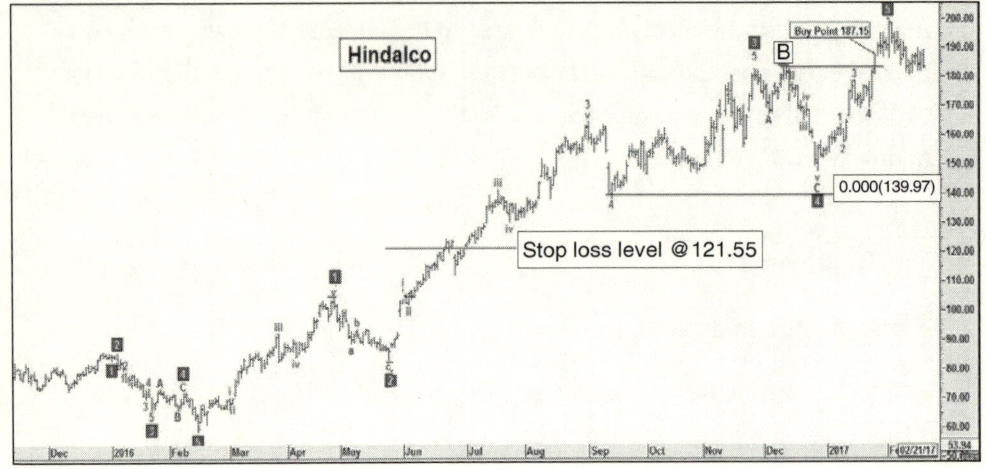

Figure 8.4: **Daily stock price chart of Hindalco**

~

At the time of writing, the stock price was trading around the buying levels. One should hold the long position with the given stop loss for price targets suggested by the Fibonacci study. If the price falls short of the upside target, then one should exit the long positions as follows:

- As and when the level made by the immediate preceding fractal iv during the earlier advance of Wave 5 is cracked on the downside, because such a break signals that the advance of Wave 5 has come to an end;
- As and when the bottom of Wave A is cracked on the downside in a down move from Wave B to Wave C;
- As and when the bottom of Wave 1 is cracked on the downside in a down move from Wave 2 to Wave 3.

At the time of writing, none of the above exit signals had emerged on the price chart, and hence one needed to stay vigilant.

Example 8.5: Tata Power

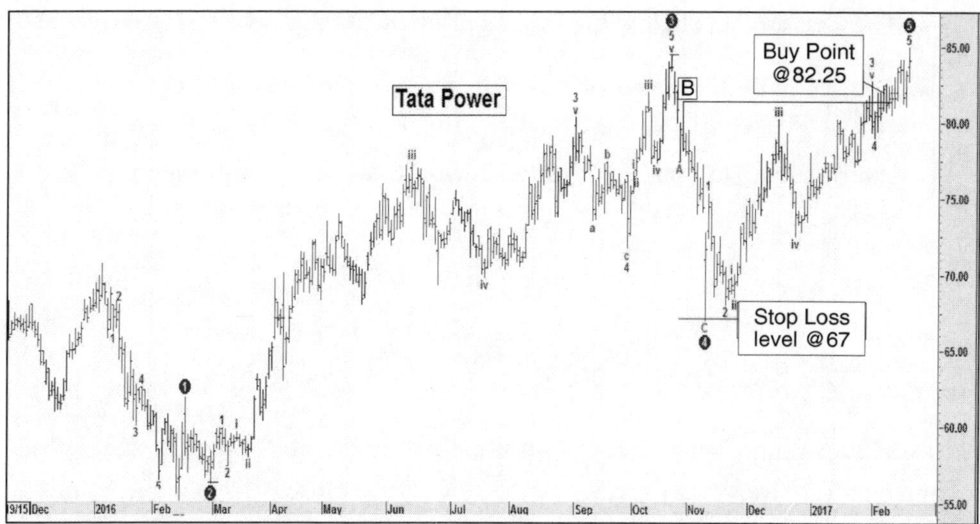

Figure 8.5: **Daily stock price chart of Tata Power**

~

Applying Elliott Wave Theory on the chart in Figure 8.5 suggests buying Tata Power as and when the stock price closes above the level made by the immediate preceding fractal B during the earlier decline of Wave 4, i.e. buying at around ₹82.25 levels. The stop loss would be placed at or below the 61.80% retracement level of Wave 3, i.e. at around ₹67 levels.

Since the length of Wave 3 is more than 1.618 times that of Wave 1, Fibonacci relationships would suggest the following:

- The first price target level for Wave 5 is ₹76, i.e. at 1.618 times the length of Wave 1;
- The second price target level for Wave 5 is ₹84, i.e. at 2.618 times the length of Wave 1.

These targets are not marked in Figure 8.5 because:

- The first target is below the buying price of ₹82.25.
- The second target level of ₹84 is just above the buying price level of ₹82.25. There is no point buying at ₹82.25 levels for a target price level around ₹84 on the upside. I would suggest avoid taking such trades.

~

Example 8.6: Tata Motors

Applying Elliott Wave Theory on the chart in Figure 8.6 would suggest buying Tata Motors as and when the stock price closes above the level of the immediate preceding fractal B made earlier by the declining Wave 4, i.e. buying at around ₹460 levels. The stop loss for this long trade would be placed at or just below the 61.80% retracement level of Wave 3, i.e. at about ₹340 levels.

Since the length of Wave 3 is more than 1.618 times that of Wave 1, Fibonacci relationships would suggest the following:

- The first price target level for Wave 5 is ₹472, i.e. at 1.618 times the length of Wave 1;

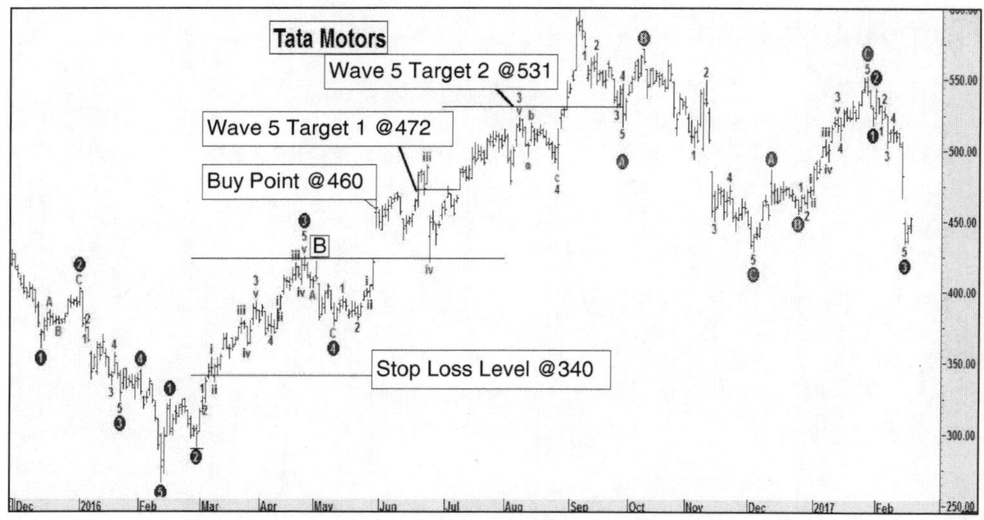

Figure 8.6: **Daily stock price chart of Tata Motors**

~

- The second price target level for Wave 5 is ₹531, i.e. at 2.618 times the length of Wave 1.

In this case, the stock price did move up to the second price target level of ₹531.

Trade Summary

- Initiate buy trade at ₹460 levels.
- Profit booking at the first price target level of ₹472 level would have resulted in a profit of 12 points.
- Profit booking at the second upside price target levels of ₹531 would have resulted in a profit of 71 points.

Example 8.7: Titan

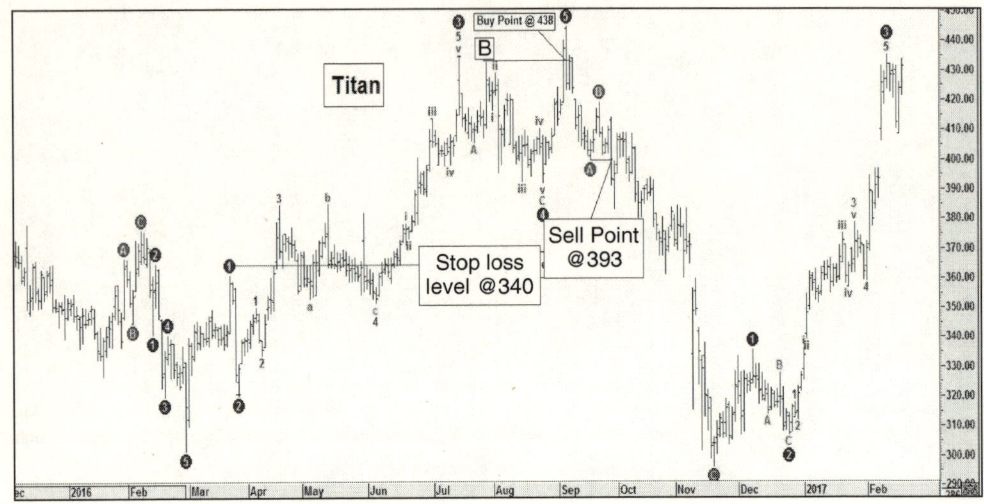

Figure 8.7: **Daily stock price chart of Titan**

~

Applying Elliott Wave Theory on the daily chart of Titan in Figure 8.7 suggests a long entry as and when the stock price closes above the level made by the immediate preceding fractal B of the declining Wave 4, i.e. buying at around ₹438 levels. The stop loss is can be placed at or below the 61.80% retracement level of Wave 3, i.e. at around ₹364 levels.

Since Wave 3 is more than 1.618 times the length of Wave 1, Fibonacci relationships would suggest the following:

- The first price target level for Wave 5 is ₹450, i.e. at 1.618 times the length of Wave 1; and
- The second price target level for Wave 5 is ₹484, i.e. at 2.618 times the length of Wave 1.

In this case, the stock price started declining immediately and cracked the bottom of Wave A on the downside during its down move from

Wave B to Wave C. As such, one should close all buy side positions as and when the bottom of Wave A is cracked on the downside, i.e. at around ₹393 levels.

Trade Summary

- Initiate buy trade at ₹438 levels.
- Closing the buy side position at the exit point, i.e. at ₹393 levels would have resulted in a loss of 45 points.

This loss of 45 points could have been recovered if one went short on the stock at ₹393 levels. This tactic is explained ahead under the topic "Selling When the Advancing Wave 5 Comes to an End" (*see* Figure 9.5).

~

Example 8.8: Cairn India

Applying Elliott Wave Theory on Figure 8.8 suggests buying as and when the stock price closes above the level made earlier by the immediate preceding fractal B during the decline of Wave 4, i.e. buying at around ₹208.50 levels. The stop loss is to be placed at or a little below the 61.80% retracement level of Wave 3, i.e. at about ₹161 level as protection against any unexpected downside.

Since the length of Wave 3 is more than 1.618 times the length of Wave 1, the Fibonacci relationship study would suggest the following:

- The first price target level for Wave 5 is ₹271, i.e. at 1.618 times the length of Wave 1; and
- The second price target level for Wave 5 is ₹324, i.e. at 2.618 times the length of Wave 1.

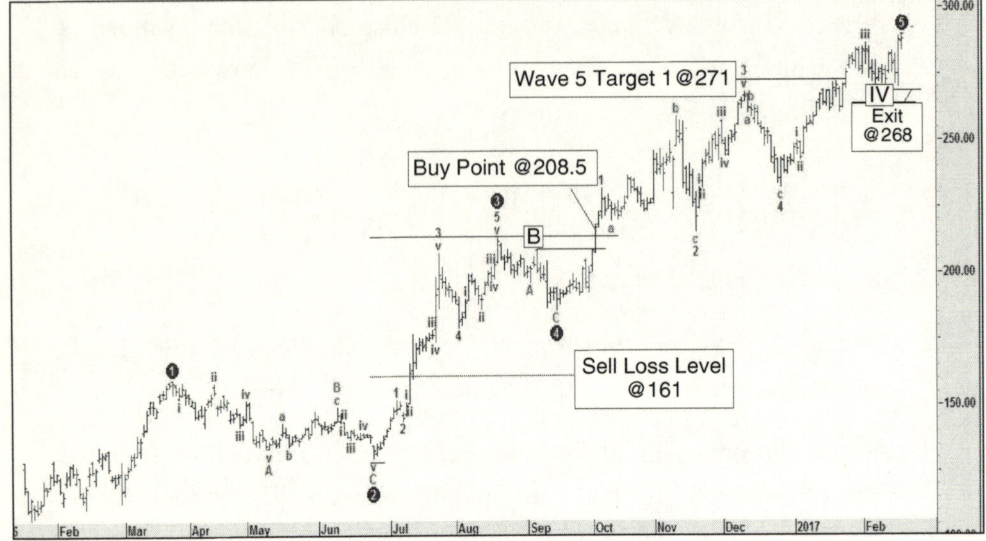

Figure 8.8: **Daily stock price chart of Cairn India**

~

The second target is not marked in Figure 8.8 as it falls outside the chart territory.

In this case, the stock price rallied to the first upside target level of ₹271. At the time of writing, the stock was trading around ₹287 while the level of the immediate preceding fractal iv of the ongoing Wave 5 was at ₹268 levels. Accordingly, one should hold on to the long position with a stop loss at ₹268 levels for the target price level of about ₹324, but exit if the price closes below ₹268 levels.

Trade Summary

- Initiate buy trade at ₹208.50 levels.
- Profit booking at the first upside price target at ₹271 level would have resulted in a profit of 62.50 points.

Example 8.9: Zee Entertainment

Figure 8.9: **Daily stock price chart of Zee Entertainment**

~

Applying Elliott Wave Theory on Figure 8.9 suggests buying Zee Entertainment as and when the stock price closes above the level made by the immediate preceding fractal B during the earlier decline of Wave 4, i.e. buying at around ₹462 levels. The buy side stop loss can be placed at or a little below 61.80% retracement level of Wave 3, i.e. at ₹408 levels.

Since the length of Wave 3 is more than 1.618 times that of Wave 1, Fibonacci relationships would suggest the following:

- The first price target level for Wave 5 is ₹526, i.e. at 1.618 times the length of Wave 1; and
- The second price target level for Wave 5 is ₹583, i.e. at 2.618 times the length of Wave 1.

As it turned out, the stock price rallied to the second price target level of ₹583 on the upside.

Trade Summary

- Initiate buy trade at ₹462 levels.
- Profit booking at the first upside price target level of ₹526 would have resulted in a profit of 64 points.
- Profit booking at the second upside price target level of ₹583 would have resulted in a profit of 131 points.

~

Example 8.10: IndusInd Bank

Applying Elliott Wave Theory on Figure 8.10 suggests buying as and when the stock price of Indusind Bank closes above the level made by the immediate preceding fractal [B] during the earlier decline of Wave 4, i.e. buying at around ₹1,131 levels. The stop loss is to be placed at below the 61.80% retracement level of Wave 3, i.e. at about ₹990 levels.

Since the length of Wave 3 is more than 1.618 times the length of Wave 1, Fibonacci relationships would suggest the following:

- The first price target level for Wave 5 is ₹1,273, i.e. at 1.618 times the length of Wave 1;
- The second price target level for Wave 5 is ₹1,411, i.e. at 2.618 times the length of Wave 1.

As it turned out, the stock price failed to rally up even to the first price target level of ₹1,273. In fact, the price first started moving sideways and thereafter began declining. The price cracked the bottom of Wave A on the downside in its down move from Wave B to Wave C. In such a case, one should exit buy side positions as and when the bottom of Wave A is cracked on the downside, i.e. sell at ₹1,093 levels in this case.

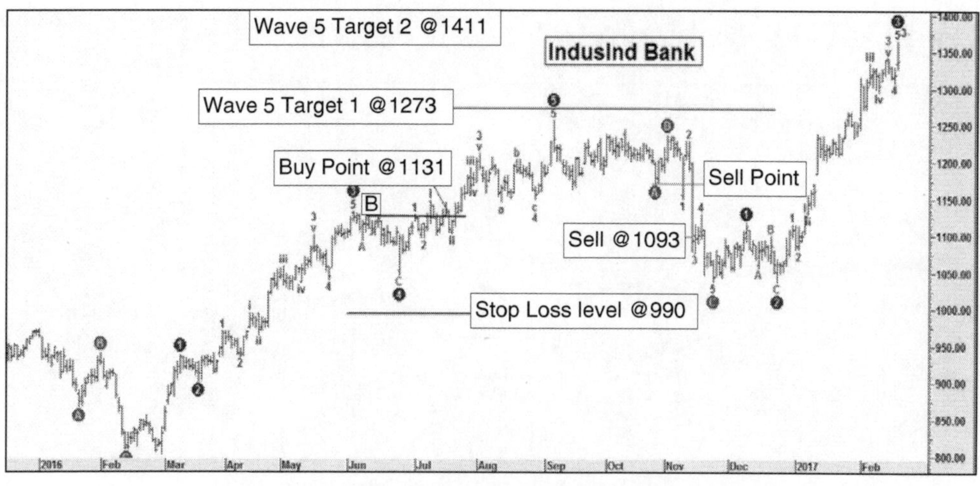

Figure 8.10: **Daily stock price chart of IndusInd Bank**

~

Trade Summary

- Initiate the buy trade at ₹1131 levels.
- Profit booking at the first upside price target level of ₹1,017 would have resulted in a profit of 88 points.
- Closing the buy side position at the exit point, i.e. at ₹1,093 levels would have resulted in a loss of 39 points.

  This loss could have been recovered by going short at ₹1,093 levels — and later going long as and when Wave 3 emerged. These two trades are also explained later in this book:

  - The selling example is explained in Figure 9.7, and
  - The buying example is explained in Figure 7.11.

Example 8.11: Mahindra Holidays & Resorts

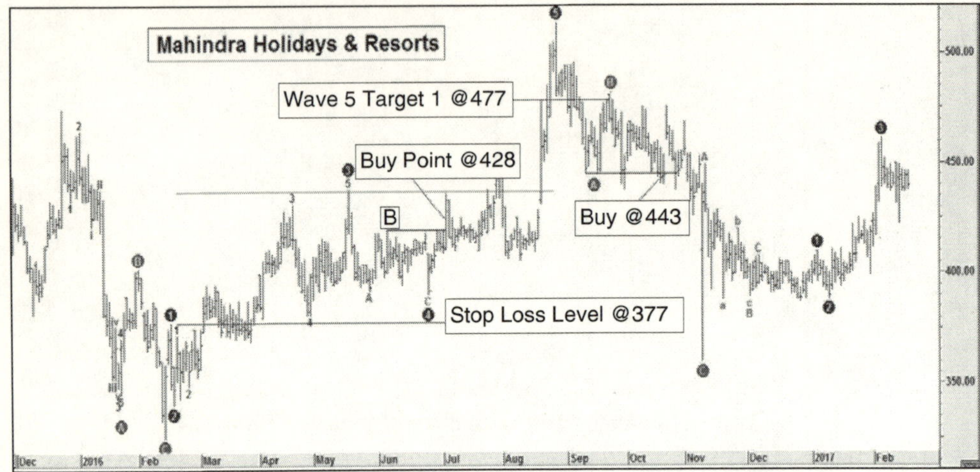

Figure 8.11: **Daily stock price chart of Mahindra Holidays & Resorts**

~

Applying Elliott Wave Theory on Figure 8.11 would have suggested buying as and when the stock price of Mahindra Holidays & Resorts closes above the level made by the immediate preceding fractal [B] during the earlier decline of Wave 4, i.e. buying at about ₹428 levels. The stop loss is to be placed at or just below the 61.80% retracement level of Wave 3, i.e. at about ₹377 levels to protect against any downside.

Since the length of Wave 3 is more than 1.618 times the length of Wave 1, Fibonacci relationships would suggest the following:

- The first price target level for Wave 5 is ₹477, i.e. at 1.618 times the length of Wave 1;
- The second price target level for Wave 5 is ₹528, i.e. at 2.618 times the length of Wave 1.

In this trade, the stock price rallied upward only till the first price target level of ₹477. The price then started a down move, and in this down move from Wave B to Wave C it cracked the bottom of Wave A. Had the trader booked profit at higher levels, it would have proved beneficial. Else, one should close all buy side positions as and when the bottom of Wave A is cracked on the downside, i.e. one should sell at around ₹443 levels.

Trade Summary

- Initiate buy trade at ₹428 level.
- Profit booking at the first upside price target level of ₹477 would have resulted in a profit of 49 points.
- Closing the buy side position at the exit point, i.e. at ₹443 levels; would have given a profit of 15 points.

~

Example 8.12: Birla Corporation

Applying Elliott Wave Theory on the price chart of Birla Corporation in Figure 8.12 suggests buying as and when the stock price closes above the level made by the immediate preceding fractal B during the earlier decline of Wave 4, i.e. buying at about ₹680 levels. The stop loss is to be placed at or just below 61.80% retracement level of Wave 3, i.e. at about ₹491 levels to protect against any unexpected downside.

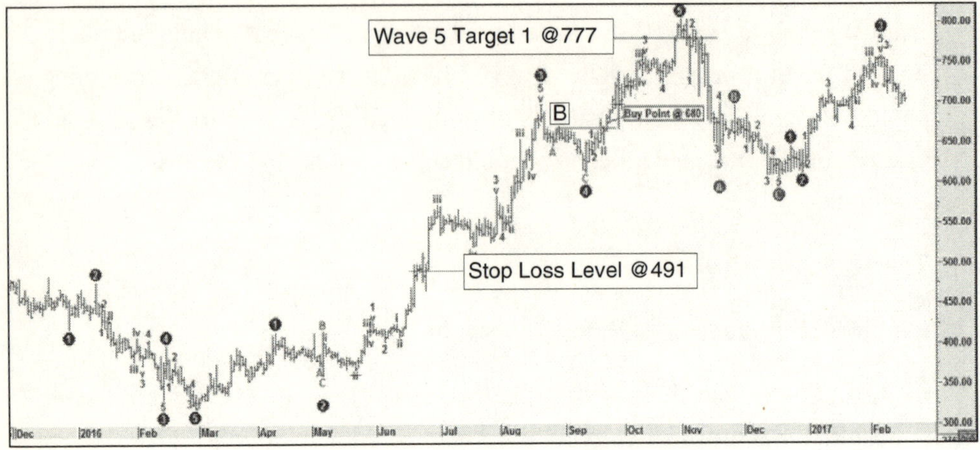

Figure 8.12: **Daily stock price chart of Birla Corporation**

~

Since the length of Wave 3 is more than 2.618 times the length of Wave 1, Fibonacci relationships would suggest locking profit at 1.618 times the length of Wave 1, i.e. at about ₹777 levels on the upside.

In this case, the stock price did rally up to the first price target level of ₹777.

Trade Summary

- Initiate buy trade at ₹680 levels.
- Profit booking at the first upside price target level of ₹777 would have resulted in a profit of 97 points.

~

Example 8.13: Eicher Motors

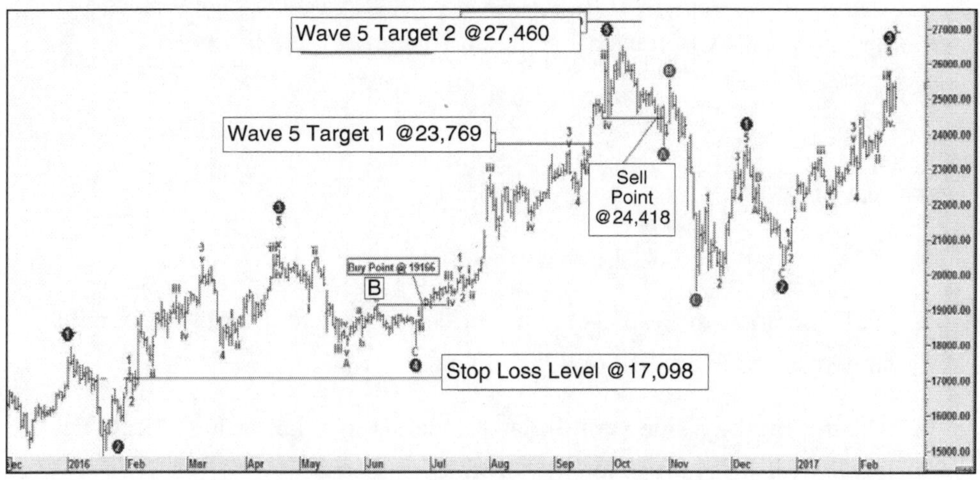

Figure 8.13: **Daily stock price chart of Eicher Motors**

~

Applying Elliott Wave Theory on the chart of Eicher Motors in Figure 8.13 suggests buying as and when the stock price closes above the level made by fractal B during the earlier the decline of Wave, i.e. buying at about ₹19,166 levels. The stop loss is to be placed at or below the 61.80% retracement level of Wave 3, i.e. at or about ₹17,098 levels to protect against any unexpected downside.

Since the length of Wave 3 is more than 1.618 times the length of Wave 1, Fibonacci relationships would suggest the following:

- The first price target level for Wave 5 is ₹23,769, i.e. at 1.618 times the length of Wave 1;
- The second price target level for Wave 5 is ₹27,460, i.e. at 2.618 times the length of Wave 1.

In this case, the stock price rallied higher only up to the first price target level of ₹23,769, and then started declining. During this down move from

Wave B to Wave C, the price cracked the bottom of Wave A on the downside. In such a case, one should exit long positions as and when the bottom of Wave A is cracked on the downside, i.e. sell at around ₹24,418 levels.

Trade Summary

- Initiate buy trade at ₹19,166 levels.
- Profit booking at the first upside price target level of ₹23,769 would have resulted in a profit of 4,603 points.
- Closing the buy side position at the exit point, i.e. at about ₹24,419 levels would have resulted in a profit of 5,252 points.

Example 8.14: Hero Motors

Applying Elliott Wave Theory on Figure 8.14 suggests buying as and when the stock price closes above the level of the immediate preceding fractal B made during the earlier decline of Wave 4, i.e. buying at about ₹2,962 levels. The stop loss is to be placed below the 61.80% retracement level of Wave 3, i.e. at about ₹2,718 levels to protect against any unexpected down.

Since the length of Wave 3 is more than 1.618 times the length of Wave 1, Fibonacci relationships would suggest the following:

- The first price target level for Wave 5 is ₹3,178, i.e. at 1.618 times the length of Wave 1;

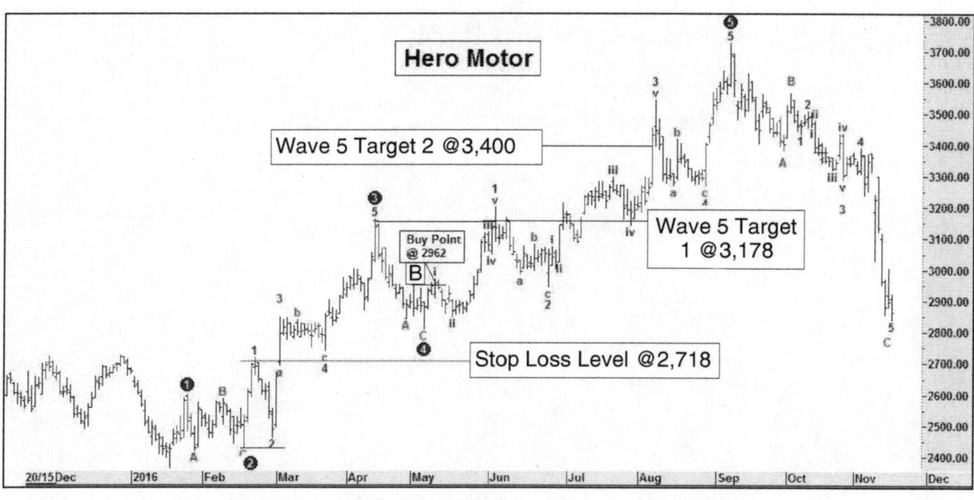

Figure 8.14: **Daily stock price chart of Hero Motors**

~

- The second price target level for Wave 5 is ₹3,400, i.e. at 2.618 times the length of Wave 1.

As it turned out, the stock price rallied up to the second price target levels of ₹3,400. In such situations, one must close all the long positions as and when the second price target is achieved.

Trade Summary

- Initiate buy trade at ₹2,962 levels.
- Profit booking at the first upside price target level of ₹3,178 would have resulted in a profit of 216 points.
- Profit booking at the second upside price target level of around ₹3,400 would have resulted in a profit of 438 points.

~

Example 8.15: Kotak Mahindra Bank

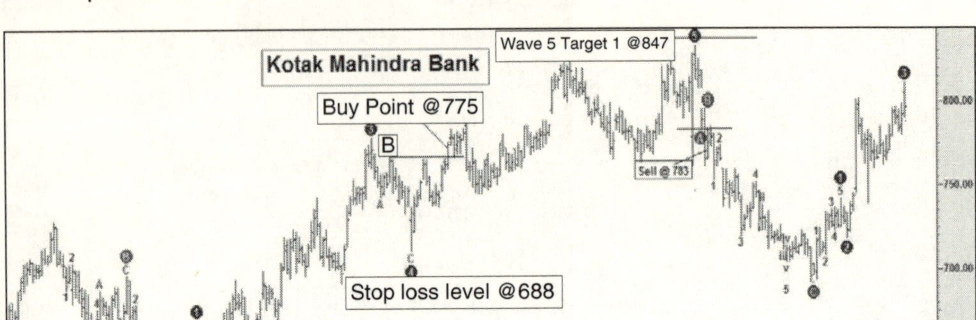

Figure 8.15: **Daily stock price chart of Kotak Mahindra Bank**

~

Applying Elliott Wave Theory on the chart of Kotak Mahindra Bank in Figure 8.15 suggests buying as and when the stock price closes above the level of the immediate preceding fractal B made during the earlier decline of Wave 4, i.e. buying at about ₹775 levels. The stop loss is to be placed at or below the 61.80% retracement level of Wave 3, i.e. at about ₹688 levels to protect against any unexpected move on the downside.

Since the length of Wave 3 is more than 1.618 times the length of Wave 1, Fibonacci relationships would suggest the following:

- The first price target level for Wave 5 is ₹846, i.e. at 1.618 times the length of Wave 1;
- The second price target level for Wave 5 is ₹927, i.e. at 2.618 times the length of Wave 1.

In this case, the stock price failed to rally even up to the first price target level of ₹846. In fact, the price started a down move from a little below

₹846 and cracked the bottom of Wave A while moving down from Wave B to Wave C. In such a case, one should close all long positions and when the bottom of Wave A is cracked on the downside, i.e. sell at ₹783 levels in this case.

Trade Summary

- Initiate buy trade at ₹775 levels.
- Closing buy side position at the exit point, i.e. at about ₹783 levels would have resulted in a profit of 8 points.

~

Example 8.16: TCS

Applying Elliott Wave Theory on the chart in Figure 8.16 suggests buying as and when the stock price closes above the level of the immediate preceding fractal [B] made earlier by the declining Wave 4, i.e. buying at about ₹2,578 levels. The stop loss should be placed at or below the 61.80% retracement level of Wave 3, i.e. at ₹2,449 levels to protect against any unexpected downside move.

In this case, we expect Wave 5 to be a weak rally as Wave 4 has retraced more than 61.80% of Wave 3. Accordingly, Fibonacci relationships suggest buying only for price target of 1.618 times the length of Wave, i.e. at about ₹2,691 levels.

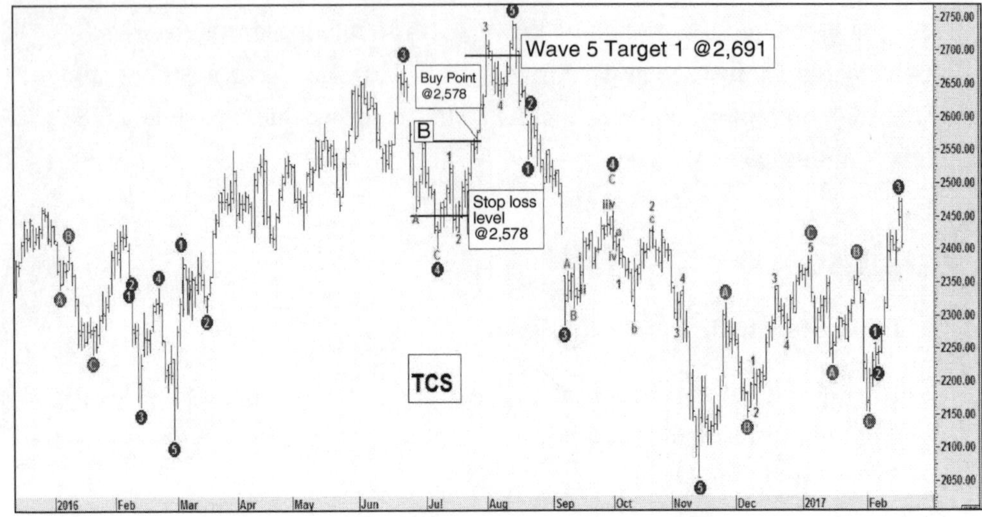

Figure 8.16: **Daily stock price chart of TCS**

~

In the event, the stock price rallied to the target price level of ₹2,691 on the upside. Since Wave 4 has retraced more than 61.80% retracement of Wave 3, one must not hold any long positions beyond this point.

Trade Summary

- Initiate buy trade at ₹2,578 levels.
- Profit booking at the first upside price target level of ₹2,691 would have resulted in a profit of 113 points.

Example 8.17: REC

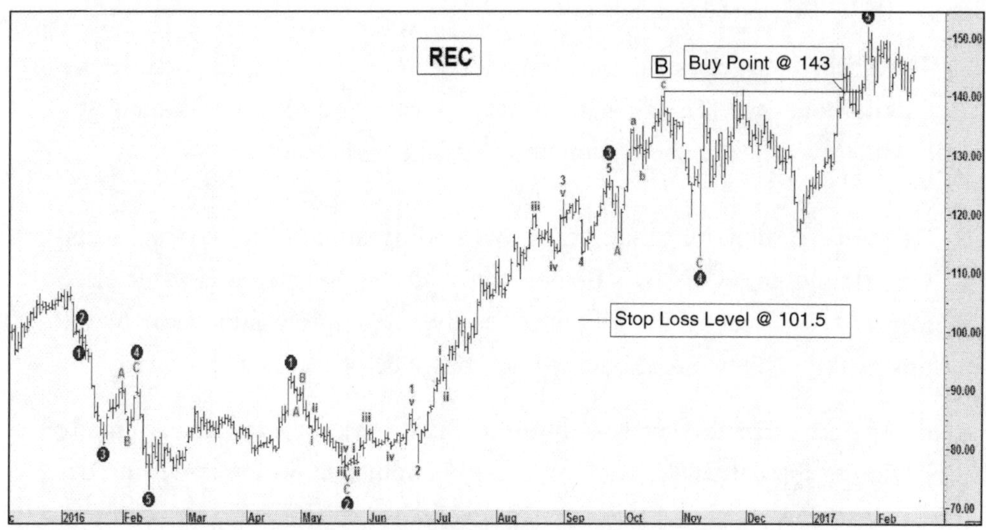

Figure 8.17: **Daily stock price chart of REC**

~

Applying Elliott Wave Theory on Figure 8.17 suggests buying as and when the stock price closes above the level of the immediate preceding fractal B made earlier during the decline of Wave 4, i.e. buying at about ₹143 levels. The stop loss is to be placed at or below the 61.80% retracement level of Wave 3, i.e. at ₹101.50 levels as protection against any unexpected down move.

Since the length of Wave 3 is more than 1.618 times that of Wave 1, Fibonacci relationships would suggest the following:

- The first price target level for Wave 5 is ₹144, i.e. at 1.618 times the length of Wave 1;

- The second price target level for Wave 5 is ₹163, i.e. at 2.618 times the length of Wave 1.

The second target is not marked in Figure 8.8 as it falls outside the chart's boundary. The first target price level of ₹144 is just around the buying level; hence, there is no point buying for this target.

At the time of writing, the price was trading around the buying levels. One should hold the buy side position with the given stop loss for price targets suggested by the Fibonacci study. If the price falls short of the upside target, then one should exit the buy side positions as follows:

- As and when the level of the immediate preceding fractal iv made during the earlier advance of Wave 5 is cracked on the downside because that's a signal that the ongoing advance of Wave 5 has come to an end.
- As and when the bottom of Wave A is cracked on the downside during any down move from Wave B to Wave C.
- As and when the bottom of Wave 1 is cracked on the downside during any down move from Wave 2 to Wave 3.

At the time of writing, none of the above exit points had emerged on the price chart, hence there is need to be vigilant.

Example 8.18: UPL

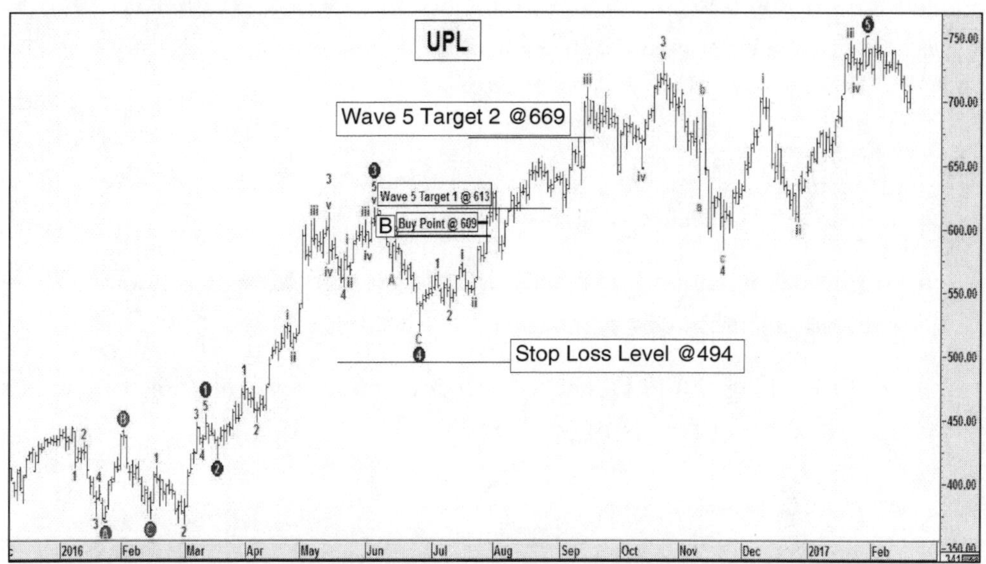

Figure 8.18: **Daily stock price chart of UPL**

~

Applying Elliott Wave Theory on the chart in Figure 8.18 would suggest buying as and when the stock price closes above the level of the immediate preceding fractal B made earlier by the declining Wave 4, i.e. buying at about ₹609 levels. The stop loss is to be placed below the 61.80% retracement level of Wave 3, i.e. at around ₹494 levels.

Since the length of Wave 3 is more than 1.618 times that of Wave 1, Fibonacci relationships would suggest the following:

- The first price target level for Wave 5 is ₹613, i.e. at 1.618 times the length of Wave 1;
- The second price target level for Wave 5 is ₹669, i.e. at 2.618 times the length of Wave 1.

As it turned out, the stock price rallied up to the second upside price target level of ₹669. In such a trade, one must close all the positions as and when this second price target is achieved.

Trade Summary

- Initiate buy trade at ₹609 levels.
- Profit booking at the first upside price target level of ₹613 would have resulted in a profit of 4 points.
- Profit booking at the second upside price target level of ₹669 would have resulted in a profit of 60 points.

~

Example 8.19: Tata Steel

Applying Elliott Wave Theory on Figure 8.19 suggests buying as and when the stock price closes above the level of the immediate preceding fractal B made during the earlier decline of Wave 4, i.e. buying at about ₹358 levels. The stop loss is to be placed below the 61.80% retracement level of Wave 3, i.e. at about ₹289 levels.

Since the length of Wave 3 is more than 1.618 times that of Wave 1, Fibonacci relationships would suggest the following:

- The first price target level for Wave 5 is ₹377, i.e. at 1.618 times the length of Wave 1;
- The second price target level for Wave 5 is ₹427, i.e. at 2.618 times the length of Wave 1.

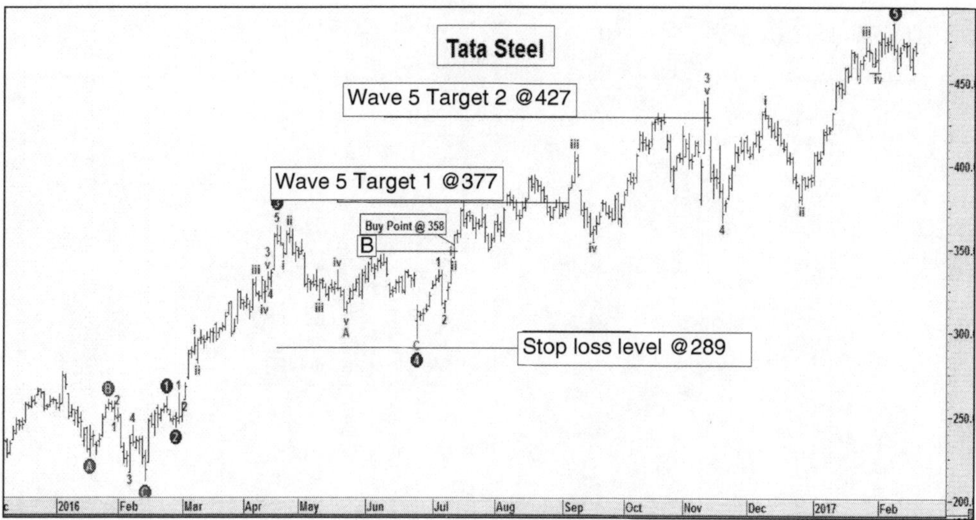

Figure 8.19: **Daily stock price chart of Tata Steel**

~

In this case, the stock price rallied up to the second price target level. One must then close all the buy positions as and when this second price target is achieved.

Trade Summary

- Initiate buy trade at ₹359 levels.
- Profit booking at the first upside price target level of ₹377 would have resulted in a profit of 18 points.
- Profit booking at the second upside price target level of ₹427 would have resulted in a profit of 68 points.

Example 8.20: IOC

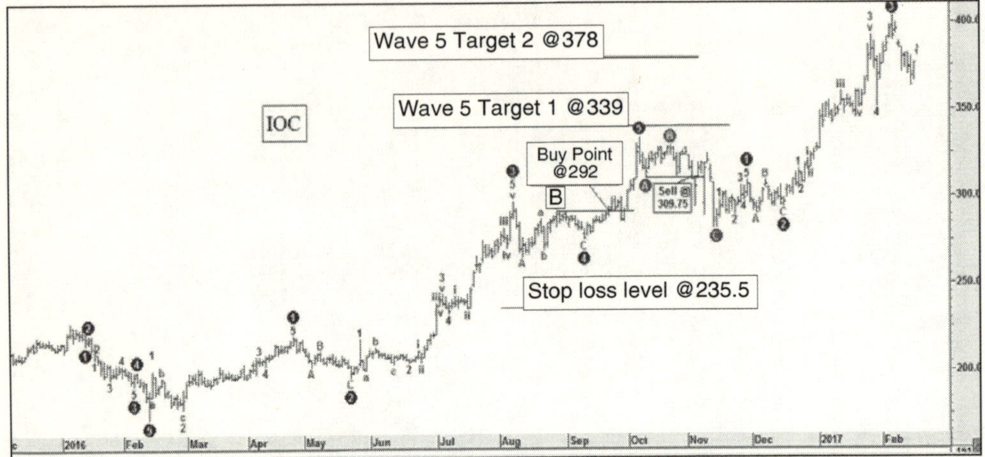

Figure 8.20: **Daily stock price chart of IOC**

~

Applying Elliott Wave Theory on IOC's chart in Figure 8.20 would suggest buying as and when the stock price closes above the level of the immediate preceding fractal B made earlier by the decline of Wave 4, i.e. buying at ₹292 levels. The stop loss is to be placed at just below the 61.80% retracement level of Wave 3, i.e. at ₹235.50 levels.

Now, since the length of Wave 3 is more than 1.618 times that of Wave 1, Fibonacci relationships would suggest the following:

- The first upside price target level for Wave 5 is ₹339, i.e. at 1.618 times the length of Wave 1;
- The second upside price target level for Wave 5 is ₹378, i.e. at 2.618 times the length of Wave 1.

In this case the stock price failed to rally even to the first price target level of ₹339. Instead, it started a down move just below ₹339 and then cracked the bottom of Wave A on its way down from Wave B to Wave

C. So one should close all the long positions as and when the bottom of Wave A is cracked on the downside, i.e. one should sell at around ₹309.75 levels.

Trade Summary

- Initiate buy trade at ₹292 levels.
- Closing the buy position at the exit point, i.e. at ₹309.75 levels, would have resulted in a profit of 17.75 points.

Selling When Wave 4 Ends in a Declining Market

Rules

- **Sell** as and when the level of the immediate preceding fractal B made during the earlier advance of Wave 4 is cracked on the downside as this signals that the ongoing Wave 4 pullback might have come to an end. If the Wave 4 pullback is less than 61.80% retracement level of Wave 3, then Wave 5 is likely to be a strong decline. Else, Wave 5 is likely to be a weak decline and the odds for its failure increase.
- When selling at the end of Wave 4, **stop loss** is to be placed above the 61.80% retracement level of Wave 3.
- Thereafter, the trader can make use of the Fibonacci relationships for predicting the Wave 5 **target**. However, if the length of Elliott Wave 3 is more than 1.618 times the length of Wave 1, and the stock price declines to the second price target levels, then one must close all sell positions and book profit.

- **Exit** should be around the Wave 5 target level suggested by Fibonacci study. Else, if the price falls short of the downside target, then one must exit sell positions as follows:
  - Exit as and when the level of the immediate preceding fractal iv made earlier during the decline of Wave 5 is cracked on the upside, because this signals that the decline of Wave 5 might have come to an end.
  - Exit as and when the top of Wave A is cracked on the upside during an up move from Wave B to Wave C.
  - Exit as and when the top of Wave 1 is cracked on the upside in an up move from Wave 2 to Wave 3.

Let's understand these rules better with the help of real life examples from Indian the stock market.

~

Example 8.21: TCS

Applying Elliott Wave Theory on Figure 8.21 suggests selling TCS as and when the stock price closes below the level of the immediate preceding fractal B made during the earlier advance of Wave 4, i.e. selling at around ₹2,304 levels. The stop loss should be placed above the 61.80% retracement level of Wave 3, i.e. at about ₹2,482 levels.

Since the length of Wave 3 is more than 1.618 times that of Wave 1, Fibonacci relationships would suggest the following:

- The first price target level for Wave 5 is ₹2,125, i.e. at 1.618 times the length of Wave 1;
- The second price target level for Wave 5 is ₹1,910, i.e. at 2.618 times the length of Wave 1. The second price target is not marked in Figure 8.21 as it falls outside the chart territory.

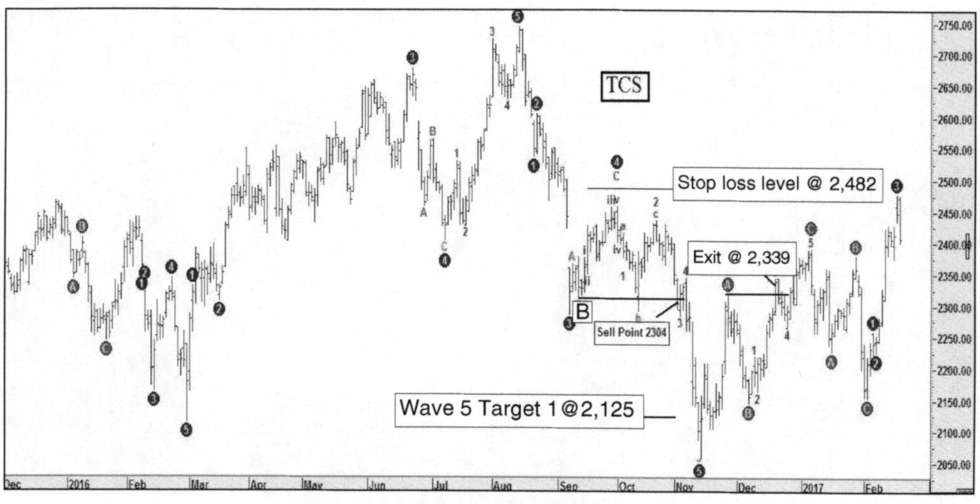

Figure 8.21: **Daily stock price chart of TCS**

~

In this case, the stock declined only till the first price target level of ₹2,125. The stock price then started moving up and cracked the top of Wave A during its up move from Wave B to Wave C. Had a trader booked profit at the lower levels, it would have proved beneficial. Else, one should close all sell positions as and when the top of Wave A is cracked on the upside, i.e. one should exit at around 2,339 levels.

Trade Summary

- Initiate sell trade at ₹2,304 levels.
- Closing the sell side position at the first downside price target level of ₹2,125 would have resulted in a profit of 179 points.
- Closing the sell side position at the exit point, i.e. at ₹2,339 levels, would have resulted in a loss of 35 points.

Example 8.22: Wipro

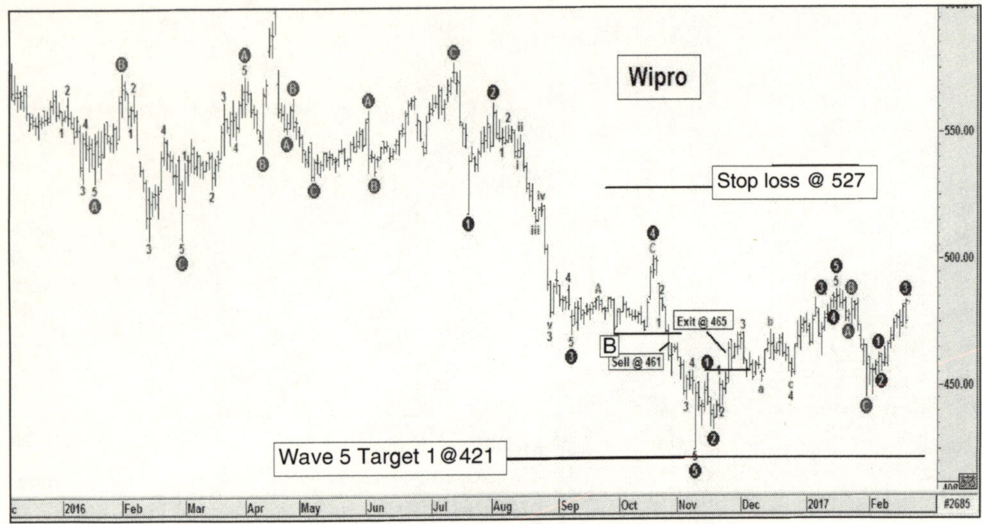

Figure 8.22: **Daily stock price chart of Wipro**

~

Applying Elliott Wave Theory on Figure 8.22 suggests selling Wipro as and when the stock price closes below the level of the immediate preceding fractal B made earlier during the advance of Wave 4, i.e. selling at about ₹461 levels. The stop loss can be placed above the 61.80% retracement level of Wave 3, i.e. at about ₹527 levels, as protection against any unexpected up move.

Since the length of Wave 3 is more than 1.618 times that of Wave 1, Fibonacci relationships would suggest the following:

- The first price target level for Wave 5 is ₹421, i.e. at 1.618 times the length of Wave 1.
- The second price target level for Wave 5 is ₹374, i.e. at 2.618 times the length of Wave 1.

The second price target of around ₹374 levels is not marked in the chart in Figure 8.22 as it falls outside the chart's range.

As it turned out, the stock price declined in the beginning but later started moving up and cracked the top of Wave 1 on the upside during its up move from Wave 2 to Wave 3. In such a case, one should close all short positions when the top of Wave 1 is cracked on the upside, i.e. in this case one should exit at ₹465 levels.

Trade Summary

- Initiate sell trade at ₹461 levels.
- Closing the sell position at the exit point, i.e. at about ₹465 levels, would have resulted in a loss of 4 points.

~

Example 8.23: Hexaware

Applying Elliott Wave Theory on Figure 8.23 suggests selling Hexaware as and when the stock price closes below the level of the immediate preceding fractal B made earlier during the advance of Wave 4, i.e. selling at around ₹208 levels. The stop loss can be placed above the 61.80% retracement level of Wave 3, i.e. at about ₹204 levels as protection against any unexpected up move.

Since the length of Wave 3 is more than 1.618 times the Wave 1, Fibonacci relationships would suggest the following:

- The first price target level for Wave 5 is ₹189, i.e. at 1.618 times the length of Wave 1.
- The second price target level for Wave 5 is ₹160, i.e. at 2.618 times the length of Wave 1.

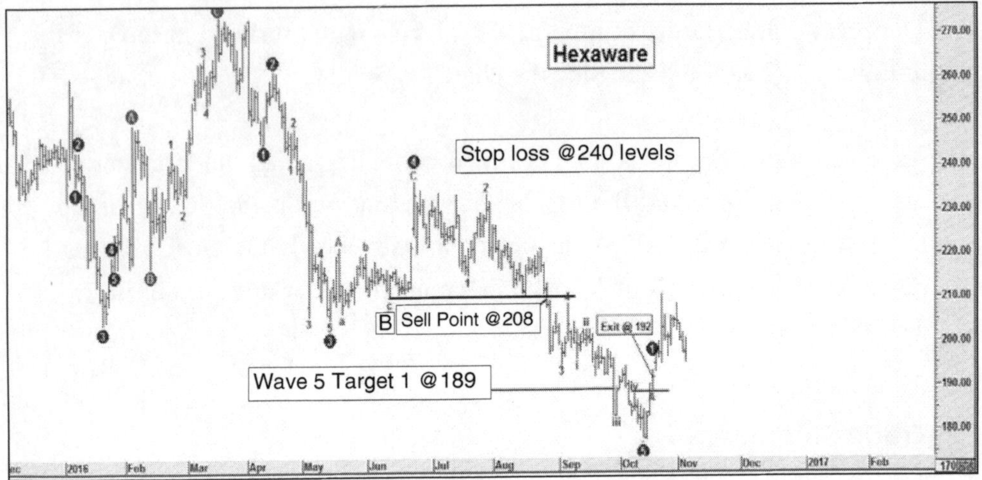

Figure 8.23: **Daily stock price chart of Hexaware**

~

The second price target level of ₹160 is not marked on the chart in Figure 8.23 as it falls outside the chart's range.

In this case, the stock price declined only to the first price target level of ₹189. The stock price then started an up move, and it cracked the top of Wave A during its up move from Wave 5 to Wave 1. It would have proved beneficial had a trader booked profits at the lower levels. Else, one should close all sell positions as and when the top of Wave A is cracked on the upside, i.e. one should exit at ₹192 levels.

Trade Summary

- Initiate sell trade at ₹208 levels.
- Profit booking at the first downside price target level of ₹189 would have resulted in a profit of 19 points.
- Closing the sell side position at the exit point, i.e. at about ₹192 levels, would have resulted in a profit of 16 points.

Example 8.24: Intellect Design Arena

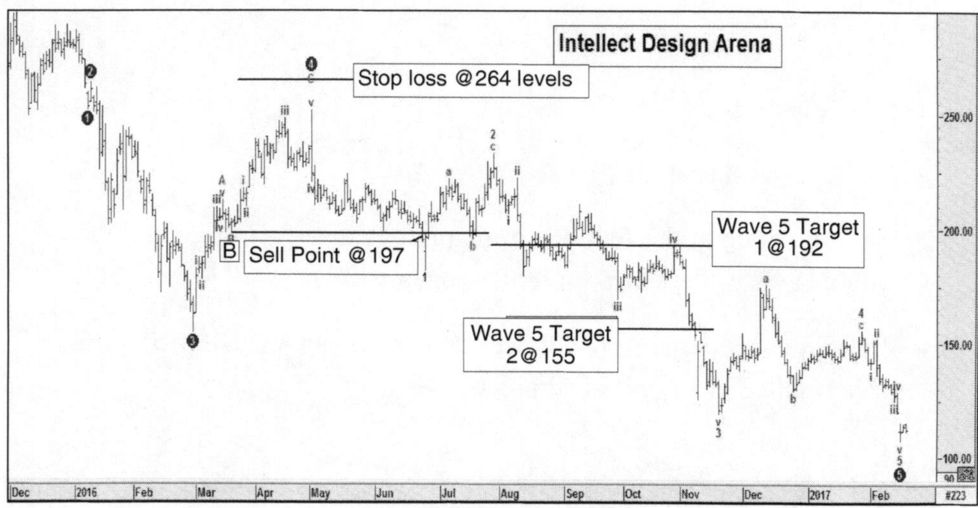

Figure 8.24: **Daily stock price chart of Intellect Design Arena**

~

Applying Elliott Wave Theory on the chart in Figure 8.24 suggests selling as and when the stock price closes below the level of the immediate preceding fractal B made earlier during the advance of Wave 4, i.e. selling at about ₹197 levels. The stop loss can be placed above the 61.80% retracement level of Wave 3, i.e. at about ₹264 levels as protection against any unexpected up move.

Since the length of Wave 3 is more than 1.618 times that of Wave 1, Fibonacci relationships would suggest the following:

- The first price target level for Wave 5 is ₹192, i.e. at 1.618 times the length of Wave 1.
- The second price target level for Wave 5 is ₹155, i.e. at 2.618 times the length of Wave 1.

In fact, the stock price declined much below the second price target level of ₹155.

Trade Summary

- Initiate sell trade at ₹197 levels.
- Profit booking at the first downside price target level of around ₹192 would have resulted in a profit of 5 points.
- Profit booking at the second downside price target level of ₹155 would have resulted in a profit of 42 points.

~

Example 8.25: DEN Networks

Applying Elliott Wave Theory on the chart in Figure 8.25 suggests selling as and when the stock price closes below the level of the immediate preceding fractal B made earlier during the advance of Wave 4, i.e. selling at about ₹81 levels. The stop loss is to be placed above the 61.80% retracement level of Wave 3, i.e. at ₹94 levels as protection against any unexpected up move.

Since the length of Wave 3 is more than 1.618 times that of Wave 1, Fibonacci relationships would suggest the following:

- The first price target level for Wave 5 is ₹83, i.e. at 1.618 times the length of Wave 1.
- The second price target level for Wave 5 is ₹72, i.e. at 2.618 times the length of Wave 1.

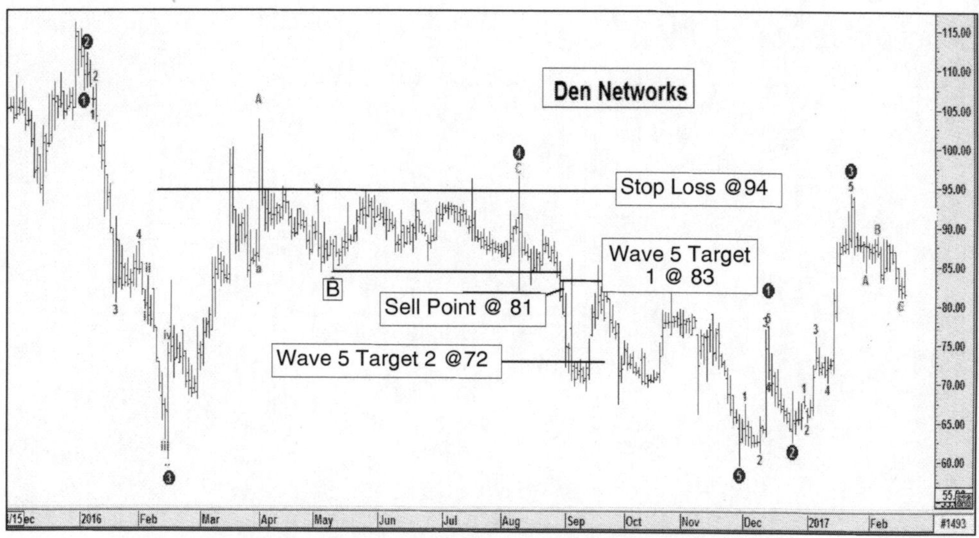

Figure 8.25: **Daily stock price chart of DEN Networks**

~

Here, the first price target level of ₹83 is above the selling level of ₹81. Hence, one cannot sell for the target price of ₹83. Moreover, the Wave 4 pullback represents more than 61.80% retracement level of Wave 3, so the price decline during Wave 5 is expected to be weak. One should, therefore, sell only if one is confident that the stock price would decline to the second price target level of ₹72. As it turned out, the stock price declined much beyond the second price target level of ₹72.

Trade Summary

- Initiate sell trade at ₹81 levels.
- Profit booking at the second downside price target level of ₹71 would have resulted in a profit of 9 points.

Example 8.26: Atul Auto

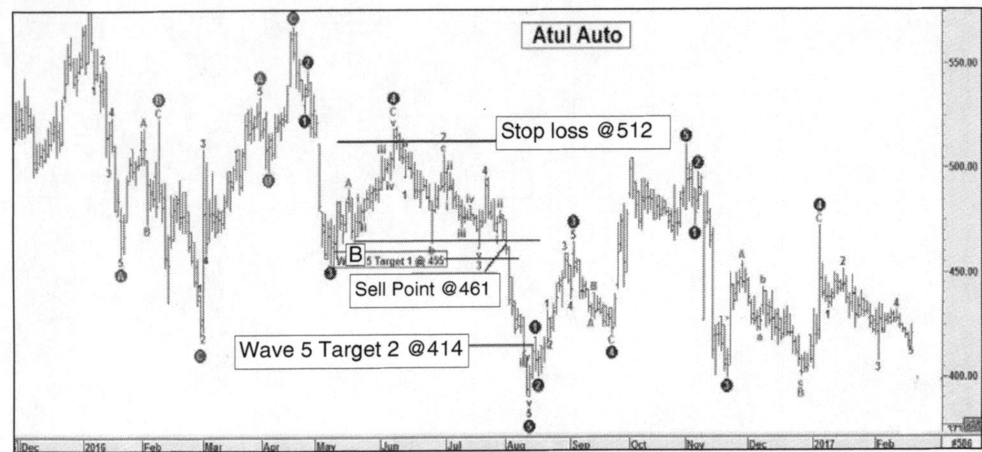

Figure 8.26: **Daily stock price chart of Atul Auto**

~

Applying Elliott Wave Theory on Figure 8.26 suggests selling Atul Auto as and when the stock price closes below the level of the immediate preceding fractal B made earlier during the advance of Wave 4, i.e. selling at around ₹461 levels. The stop loss is to be placed above the 61.80% retracement level of Wave 3, i.e. at ₹512 levels as protection against any unexpected up move.

Since the length of Wave 3 is more than 1.618 times that of Wave 1, Fibonacci relationships would suggest the following:

- The first price target level for Wave 5 is ₹455, i.e. at 1.618 times the length of Wave 1;
- The second price target level for Wave 5 is ₹414, i.e. at 2.618 times the length of Wave 1.

In this case, the first downside price target level of ₹455 is just below the selling point; hence one should not initiate a sell trade for the target price levels of ₹455. Moreover, the size of the Wave 4 pullback in this case is more than the 61.80% retracement level of Wave 3, and so the price decline in Wave 5 is expected to be a weak one. Accordingly, one should sell only if one is confident that the stock price would decline to the second price target of level ₹414.

As it turned out, the stock price declined only a little below the second price target level of ₹414.

Trade Summary

- Initiate sell trade at ₹461 levels.
- Profit booking at the second downside price target levels of ₹414 would have resulted in a profit of 47 points.

~

Example 8.27: IPCA Laboratories

Applying Elliott Wave theory on the chart in Figure 8.27 would suggest selling as and when the stock price closes below the bottom of Wave 3, i.e. selling at around ₹501 levels. The stop loss is to be placed above the 61.80% retracement level of Wave 3, i.e. at about ₹667 levels. Wave fractals A, B and C are not marked for Wave 4 as Wave 4 was just a quick pullback which ended suddenly. In such scenarios — where fractals A, B and C are not marked for Wave 4, — one should sell as and when the bottom of Wave 3 is taken off.

Since the length of Wave 3 is more than 1.618 times that of Wave 1, Fibonacci relationships would suggest the following:

- The first price target level for Wave 5 is ₹512, i.e. at 1.618 times the length of Wave 1;

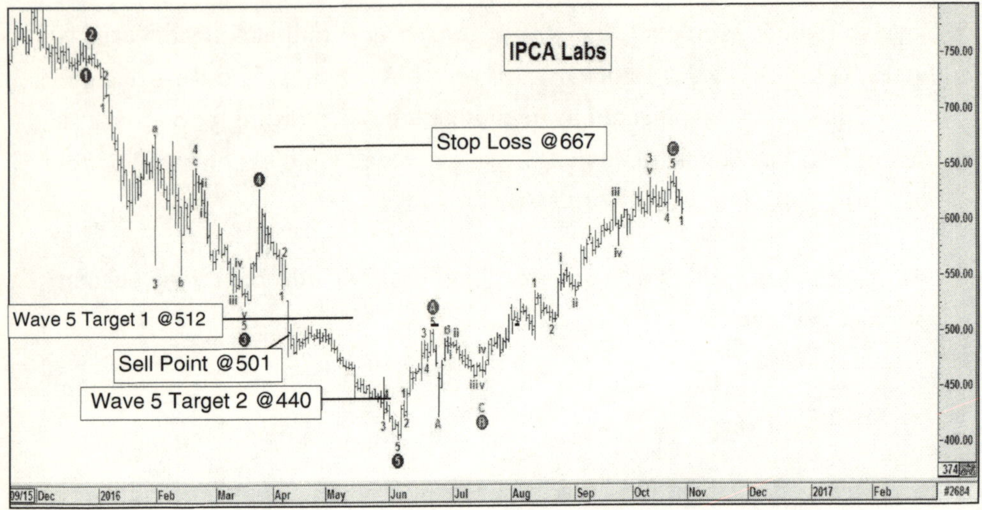

Figure 8.27 **Daily stock price chart of IPCA Laboratories**

~

- The second price target level for Wave 5 is ₹440, i.e. at 2.618 times the length of Wave 1.

Here, the first price target level of ₹512 is above the selling level of ₹501, hence one cannot sell for the target price of ₹512. As it turned out, the stock price declined just a little below the second downside target level of ₹440.

Trade Summary

- Initiate sell trade at ₹501 levels.
- Profit booking at the second downside price target level of ₹440 would have resulted in a profit of 61 points.

~

Example 8.28: Snowman Logistics

Figure 8.28: **Daily stock price chart of Snowman Logistics**

~

Applying Elliott Wave Theory on Figure 8.28 suggests selling Snowman as and when the stock price closes below the level of fractal B made earlier during the advance of Wave 4, i.e. selling at about ₹67.50 levels. The stop loss is to be placed above the 61.80% retracement level of Wave 3, i.e. at about ₹79 levels to protect against any unexpected move on the upside.

Since the length of Wave 3 is more than 1.618 times that of the Wave 1, Fibonacci relationships would suggest the following:

- The first price target level for Wave 5 is ₹59.50, i.e. at 1.618 times the length of Wave 1;
- The second price target level for Wave 5 is ₹51, i.e. at 2.618 times the length of Wave 1.

As it turned out, the stock price declined to just a little below the second price target level of ₹51.

Trade Summary

- Initiate sell trade at ₹67.50 levels.
- Profit booking at the first downside price target level of ₹59.50 would have resulted in a profit of 8 points.
- Profit booking at the second downside price target level of ₹51 would have resulted in a profit of 16.50 points.

~

Example 8.29: VRL Logistics

Applying Elliott Wave Theory on the chart in Figure 8.29 suggests selling as and when the stock price closes below the level of fractal B made during the earlier advance of Wave 4, i.e. selling at about ₹280 levels. The stop loss is to be placed above the 61.80% retracement level of Wave 3, i.e. at ₹352 levels, as protection against any unexpected up move.

Since the length of Wave 3 is more than 1.618 times that of Wave 1, the Fibonacci relationship study would suggest the following:

- The first price target level for Wave 5 is ₹274, i.e. at 1.618 times the length of Wave 1;
- The second price target level for Wave 5 is ₹234, i.e. at 2.618 times the length of Wave 1.

The first price target level of ₹274 is just below the selling point of ₹280; hence one should not initiate a sell trade if one is looking at the price target level of ₹274. As it turned out, the stock prices declined to the second price target of ₹234 level.

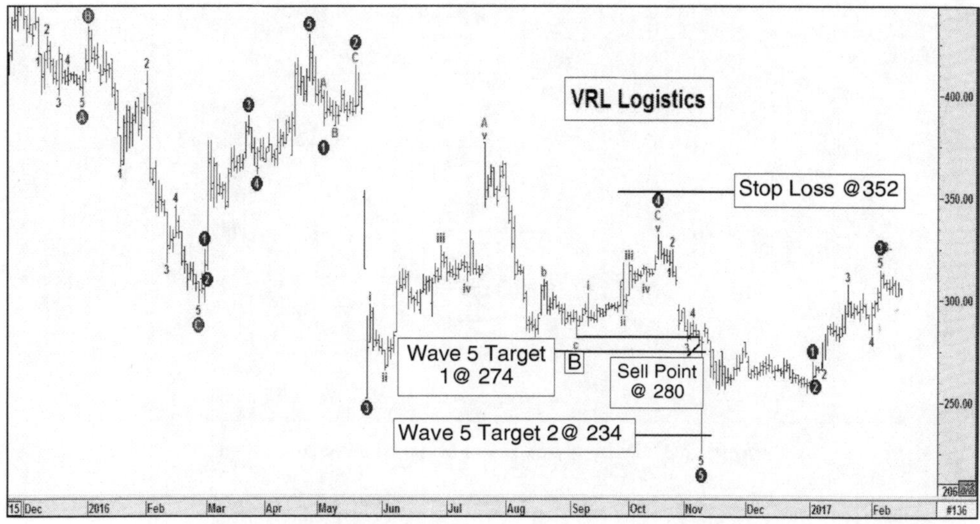

Figure 8.29: **Daily stock price chart of VRL Logistics**

~

Trade Summary

- Initiate sell trade at ₹280 levels.
- Profit booking at the second downside price target level of ₹234 would have resulted in a profit of 46 points.

~

Example 8.30: Welspun Corp

Applying Elliott Wave Theory on Figure 8.30 would suggest selling Welspun as and when the stock price closes below the level made by fractal B during the earlier advance of Wave 4, i.e. selling at around ₹78.20 levels. The stop loss is to be placed above the 61.80% retracement level of Wave 3, i.e. at ₹92.85 levels.

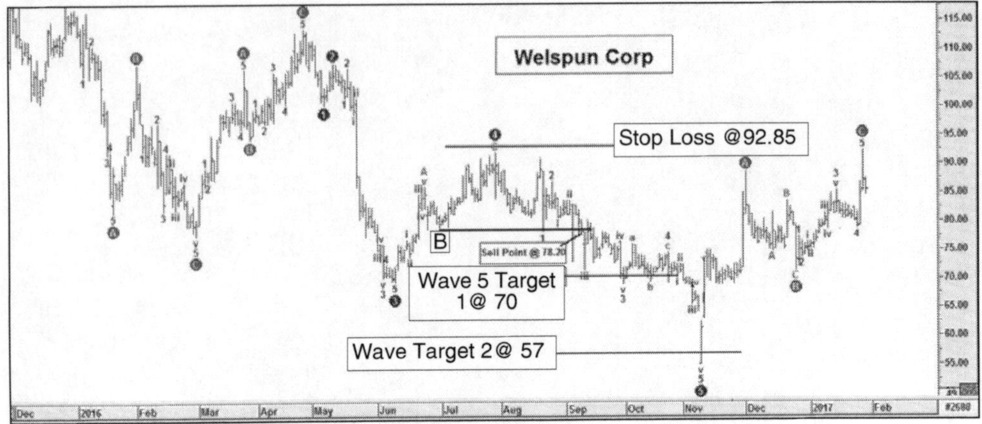

Figure 8.30: **Daily stock price chart of Welspun Corp**

~

Since the length of Wave 3 is more than 1.618 times that of Wave 1, Fibonacci relationships would suggest the following:

- The first price target for Wave 5 is ₹70 levels, i.e. at 1.618 times the length of Wave 1;
- The second price target for Wave 5 is ₹57 levels, i.e. at 2.618 times the length of Wave 1.

In this case, the stock price declined to the second price target level of ₹57.

Trade Summary

- Initiate sell trade at ₹78.20 levels.
- Profit booking at the first downside price target level at ₹70 would have resulted in a profit of 8.20 points.
- Profit booking at the second downside price target at ₹57 levels would have resulted in a profit of 21.20 points.

9

Strategy 3: Trading in the Direction of the Dominant Trend When Wave 5 Ends

The third strategy of trading in the direction of the dominant trend when Wave 5 comes to an end can be further subdivided into two parts:

1. Selling when Wave 5 comes to an end in an advancing market.

2. Buying when Wave 5 comes to an end in a declining market.

Selling When Wave 5 Ends in an Advancing Market

Rules

- Sell as and when the level of the immediate Elliott Wave fractal "iv" made during the earlier advance of Wave 5 is cracked on the downside. Before selling, however, one most make sure that the price is close to the Wave 5 target suggested by Fibonacci relationships. Else, the chances of a price decline reduce. The stop loss should be placed above the highs of Wave 5, and the sell target is the bottom of Wave 4, i.e. one should exit as and when the price falls close to the bottom of Wave 4. If the stock price decline doesn't reach this downside target and the price starts rallying instead, then one needs to keep an eye on the new wave count which might emerge at that stage — and exit accordingly. This is because a new wave count might signal that the ongoing price decline has come to an end.

- Thereafter, one should make use of Fibonacci relationships in predicting the Wave C targets. Most times Wave C halts at around the bottom of Wave 4, hence one should book profit around the bottom of Wave 4. If the stock price doesn't fall enough to reach the downside target but starts rallying back up instead, one must keep a look out for a new wave count which might then emerge — and exit accordingly. This is because the new wave count might signal that the ongoing price decline has come to an end.

Let's now understand this scenario better with the help of real time examples from the Indian stock market.

~

Example 9.1: Asian Paints

Applying Elliott Wave Theory on the chart in Figure 9.1 suggests selling Asian Paints as and when the level of fractal iv made during the earlier advance of Wave 5 is cracked on the downside, i.e. selling at about ₹1,091 levels. The stop loss should be placed above the top of Wave 5, at around ₹1,229 level in this sell trade.

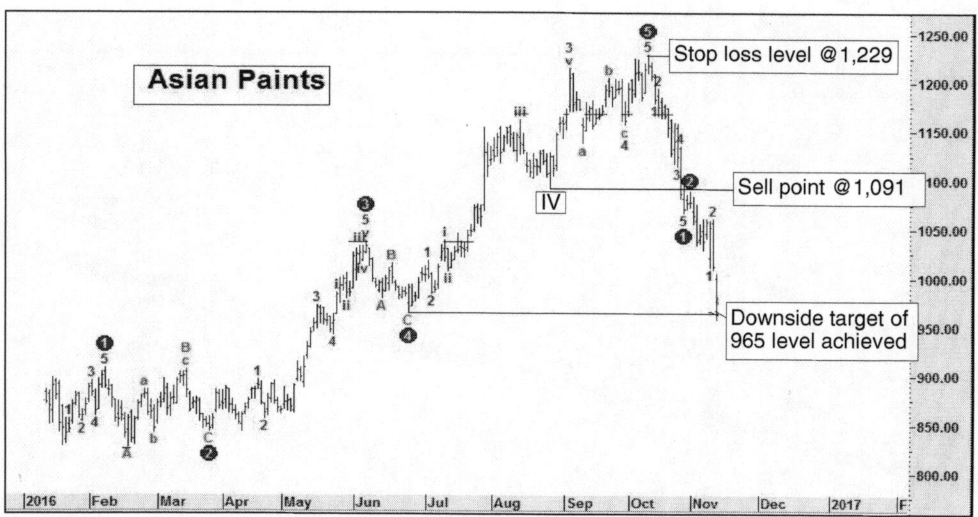

Figure 9.1: **Daily stock price chart of Asian Paints**

~

As it turned out, the stock price declined to the bottom of Wave 4 and the price target of ₹965 level was duly achieved.

Trade Summary

- Initiate sell trade at ₹1091 level.
- Profit booking at the target price level of ₹965, would have resulted in a profit of 126 points.

~

Example 9.2: BPCL

In the chart in Figure 9.2, Elliott Wave Theory would suggest selling when the level of fractal iv made during the earlier advance of Wave 5 is cracked on the downside. In other words, a sell trade can be taken at ₹597.80 levels. In this trade, the stop loss would stand above the top of Wave 5.

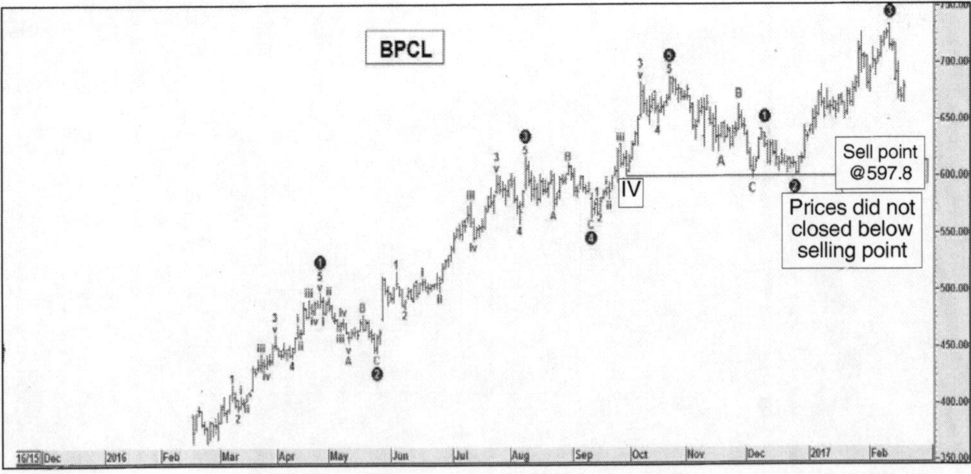

Figure 9.2: **Daily stock price chart of BPCL**

~

As it turned out, the stock price rebounded back upward and never closed below the ₹597.80 level. Thus, the sell trade never got initiated.

This example would serve to remind readers that one should only initiate a trade as and when levels being monitored are broken on closing basis, i.e. the stock price should close below the concerned level in the case of a sell trade and, conversely, the stock price should close above the concerned price level in the case of a buy trade.

~

Example 9.3: HDFC Bank

In the case of Figure 9.3, Elliott Wave Theory suggests selling as and when the bottom of Wave A is cracked during a down move from Wave B to Wave C. In other words, a sell trade would be warranted at around ₹1,211 levels. The stop loss can be placed above the top of Wave B, i.e. at around ₹1,290 levels as protection against any price downside.

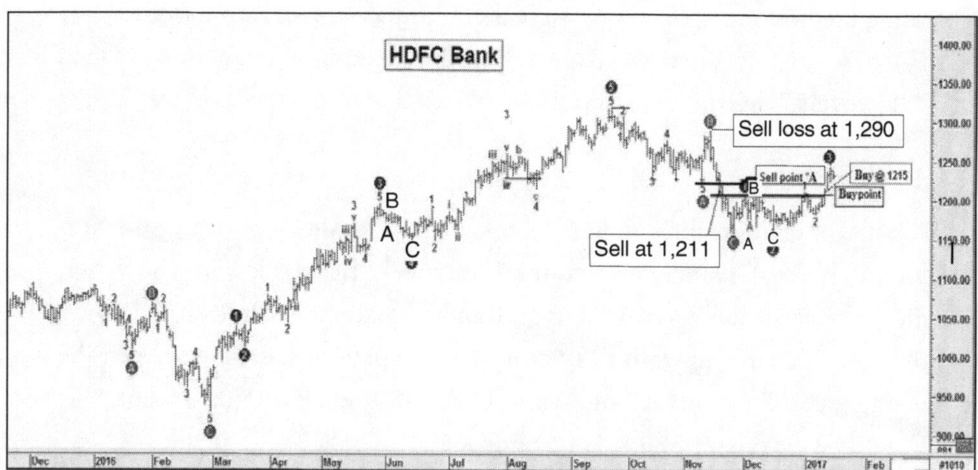

Figure 9.3: **Daily stock price chart of HDFC Bank**

~

Fibonacci relationships would suggest the downside target as the bottom of Wave 4, namely around the ₹1,145 level. The stock price, however, did not fall all the way to the target and instead started rallying. During the course of this rally, a new wave pattern got created with the emergence of an advancing Wave 3 at ₹1,215 levels. At this point, one should close all sell positions.

Trade Summary

- Initiate sell trade at ₹1,211 levels.
- Closing sell position at the exit point, i.e. at ₹1,215 levels, would have resulted in a loss of 4 points.

~

Example 9.4: Tata Motors

In the case of Figure 9.4, Elliott Wave Theory suggests selling as and when the bottom of Wave A is cracked during a down move from Wave B to Wave C. In other words, a sell trade would be warranted at around ₹513 levels. The stop loss should be placed above the top of Wave B, i.e. at ₹572 levels.

Fibonacci relationships would suggest the downside target being the bottom of Wave 4, namely around the ₹380 level. The stock price, however, did not fall all the way to the target and instead started rallying. During the course of this upward rally, a new wave pattern got formed with the emergence of the advancing Wave C at ₹487 levels. At this point, one should be closing all sell side positions.

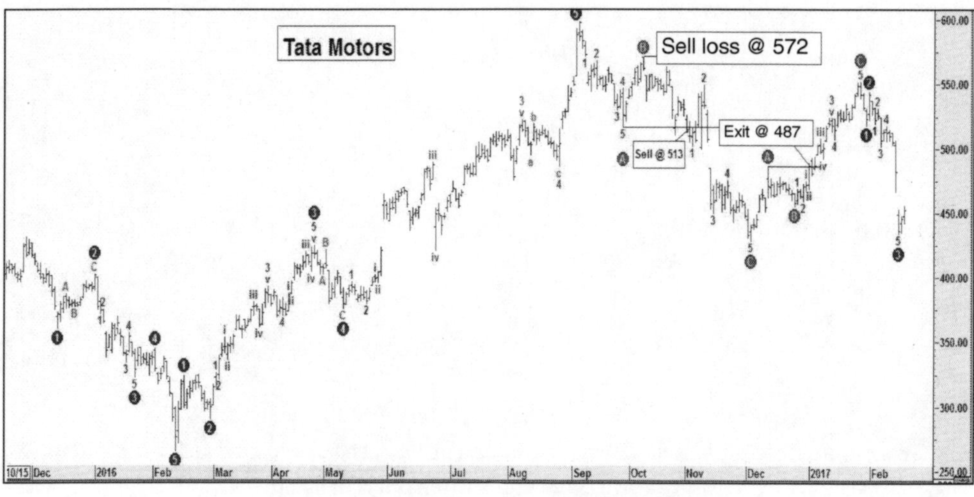

Figure 9.4: **Daily stock price chart of Tata Motors**

~

Trade Summary

- Initiate sell trade at ₹513 levels.
- Closing the sell position at the exit point, i.e. at ₹487 levels, would have resulted in a profit of 26 points.

~

Example 9.5: Titan

In the example of Figure 9.5, Elliott Wave Theory would suggest selling as and when the bottom of Wave A is cracked on the downside during a down move from Wave B to Wave C; in other words, selling at around ₹393 levels. The stop loss should be placed above the top of Wave B, namely at around ₹419 levels.

In this case, Elliott Wave practitioners would have also bought at the end of Wave 4 and incurred a loss as the then advancing Wave 5 failed to rally towards its target levels.

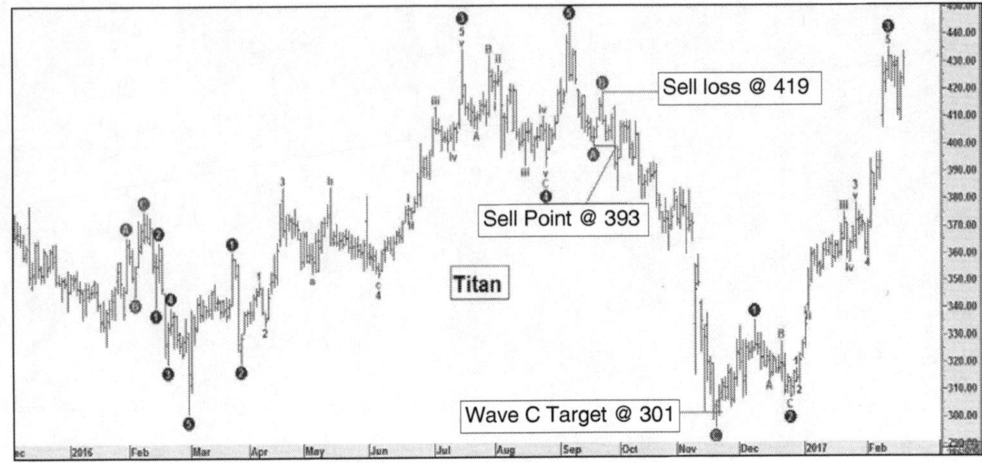

Figure 9.5: **Daily stock price chart of Titan**

~

Experience suggests that whenever Wave 5 fails to reach its target levels, the downside target for Wave C should then be 2.618 times the length of Wave A.

In this case, Fibonacci relationships would thus suggest Wave C price target at ₹301 levels, i.e. at 2.618 times the length of Wave A.

The stock price did duly decline to the price target level of ₹301 on the downside.

Trade Summary

- Initiate sell trade at ₹393 levels.
- Profit booking at price target level of ₹301 would have resulted in a profit of 92 points.

~

Example 9.6: Zee Entertainment

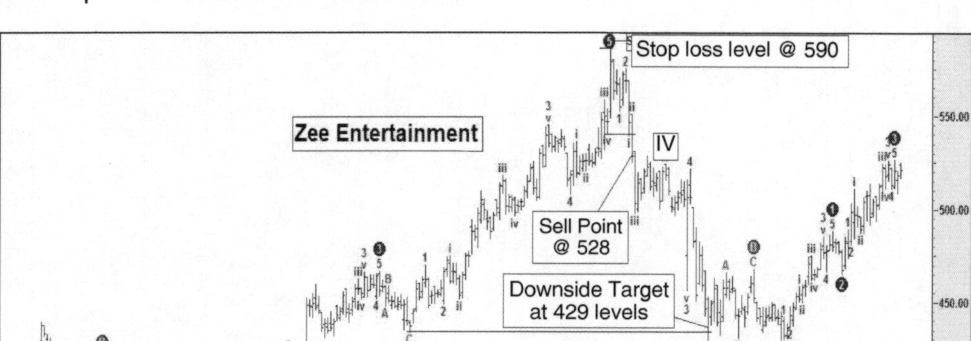

Figure 9.6: **Daily stock price chart of Zee Entertainment**

~

In the case of Figure 9.6, Elliott Wave Theory would suggest selling as and when the level made by fractal iv made during the earlier advance of Wave 5 is cracked on the downside; in other words, selling at around ₹528 levels. The stop loss should be placed above the top of Wave 5, i.e. at around ₹590 levels.

As it turned out, the stock price did decline till the bottom of Wave 4, i.e. to ₹439 levels.

Trade Summary

- Initiate sell trade at ₹528 levels.
- Profit booking at the price target level of about ₹439 would have resulted in a profit of 89 points.

Example 9.7: IndusInd Bank

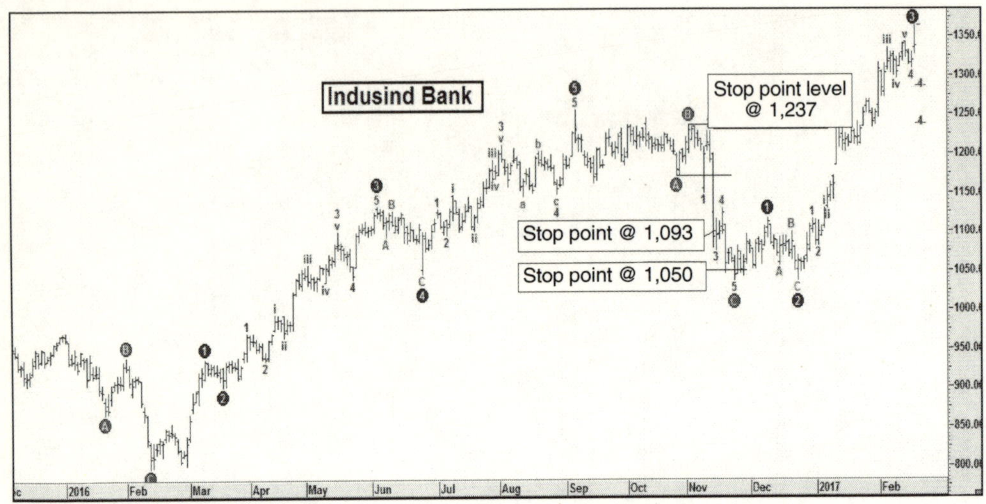

Figure 9.7: **Daily stock price chart of IndusInd Bank**

~

Analysing Figure 9.7 with the help of Elliott Wave Theory suggests a sell trade as and when the level of the bottom of Wave A is cracked in the down move from Wave B to Wave C, i.e. selling at around ₹1,093 levels. The stop loss can be placed above the top of Wave B, namely at about ₹1,237 levels.

Elliott Wave practitioners who bought at the end of Wave 4 would have incurred a loss as the advancing Wave 5 failed to rally towards its target levels. Experience suggests that whenever Wave 5 fails to rally to its target levels, the downside target for Wave C should then be 2.618 times the length of Wave A.

Fibonacci relationships in this case would suggest that Wave C price target should be around ₹1,050 level, namely at 2.618 times the length of Wave A. As it turned out, the stock price did fall to the price target levels of ₹1,050.

Trade Summary

- Initiate sell trade at ₹1,093 levels.
- Profit booking at the price target level of ₹1,050 would have resulted in a profit of 92 points.

~

Example 9.8: Mahindra Holidays & Resorts

In the example illustrated in Figure 9.8, Elliott Wave Theory would suggest selling as and when the level of the bottom of Wave A is cracked during a down move from Wave B to Wave C; in other words, selling at around ₹443 levels. The stop loss can be placed above the top of Wave B, i.e. at about ₹481 levels.

Fibonacci relationships would suggest the downside target to be the bottom of Wave 4, i.e. at around ₹387 levels and the stock price did fall to this level.

Figure 9.8: **Daily stock price chart of Mahindra Holidays & Resorts**

~

Trade Summary

- Initiate sell trade at ₹443 levels.
- Profit booking at the price target level of ₹387 would have resulted in a profit of 56 points.

~

Example 9.9: Birla Corporation

In the case of Figure 9.9, Elliott Wave Theory would suggest initiating a sell trade as and when the level made by fractal iv during the earlier advance of Wave 5 is cracked on the downside. In other words, initiating a sell trade at around ₹714 levels. The stop loss is to be placed above the top of Wave 5, i.e. at about ₹804 levels.

The stock price dutifully declined to the bottom of Wave, 4, i.e. it achieved the price target levels of ₹613.

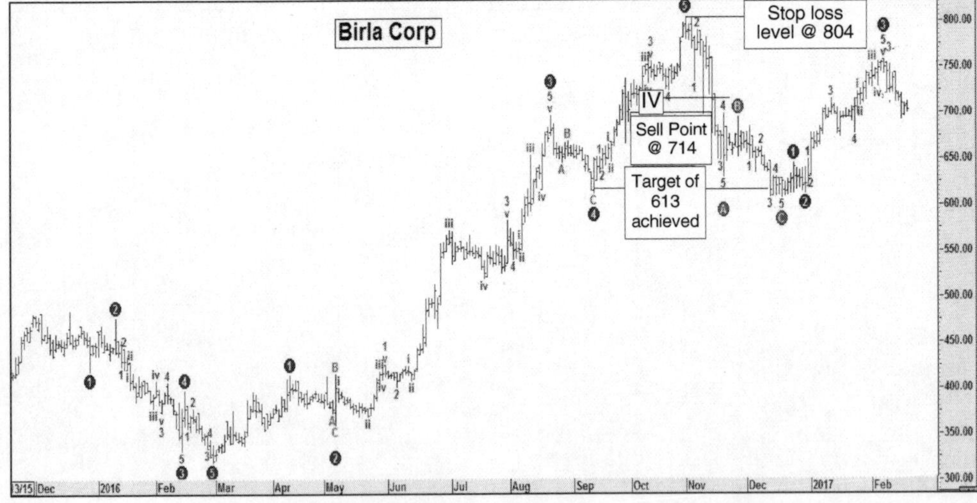

Figure 9.9: **Daily stock price chart of Birla Corporation**

~

Trade Summary

- Initiate sell trade at ₹714 levels.
- Profit booking at the downside price target levels of ₹613 would have resulted in a profit of 101 points.

~

Example 9.10: Eicher Motors

In the case of Figure 9.10, Elliott Wave Theory would suggest selling as and when the level of fractal iv made during the earlier advance of Wave 5 is cracked on the downside; i.e. selling at around ₹24,418 levels. The stop loss should be placed above the top of Wave 5, i.e. at about ₹26,641 levels.

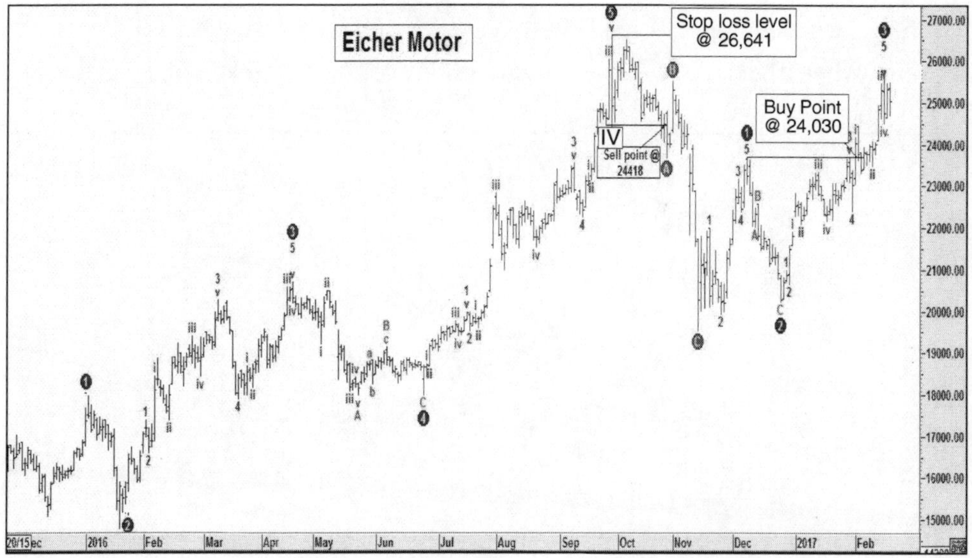

Figure 9.10: **Daily stock price chart of Eicher Motors**

~

Fibonacci relationships would suggest the bottom of Wave 4 as the downside target, i.e. around ₹18,100 levels. But the stock price did not reach the target and instead started rallying upward. During the course of this rally, a new wave pattern emerged at ₹24,030 levels in the shape of an advancing Wave 3. At this point, one should close all sell positions.

Trade Summary

- Initiate sell trade at ₹24,418 levels.
- Profit booking at ₹24,030 levels, short of the price target. Result — a profit of 388 points.

~

Example 9.11: Hero Motors

In the case of Figure 9.11, Elliott Wave Theory would suggest selling as and when the level of the bottom of Wave A is cracked during the

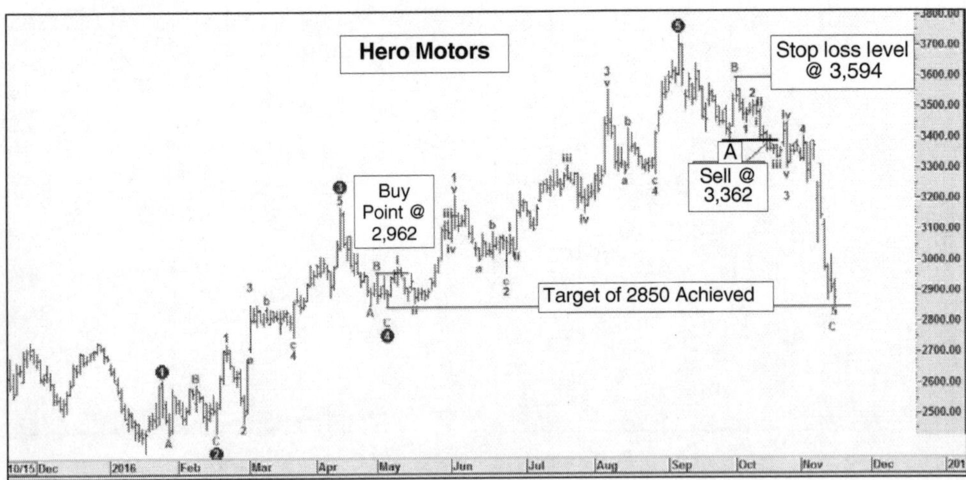

Figure 9.11: **Daily stock price chart of Hero Motors**

~

subsequent down move from Wave B to Wave C; i.e. selling at around ₹3,362 levels. The stop loss is to be placed above the top of Wave B, i.e. at ₹3,594 levels.

Fibonacci relationships would suggest the bottom of Wave 4, i.e. ₹2,850 levels, as the downside target. The stock duly declined to this price target.

Trade Summary

- Initiate sell trade at ₹3362 levels.
- Profit booking at price target level of ₹2,850 would have result in a profit of 512 points.

~

Example 9.12: Kotak Mahindra Bank

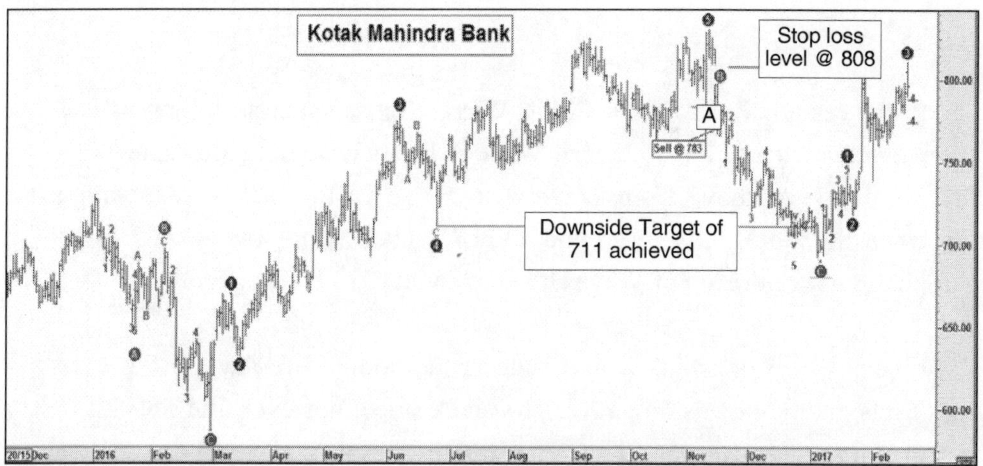

Figure 9.12: **Daily stock price chart of Kotak Mahindra Bank**

~

In the case of Figure 9.12, Elliott Wave Theory would suggest initiating a sell as and when the level of the bottom of Wave A is cracked in the subsequent down move from Wave B to Wave C. In other words, selling at around ₹783 levels. The stop loss should be placed above the top of Wave B, i.e. at around ₹808.

Fibonacci relationships would suggest the downside target as the bottom of Wave 4, i.e. about ₹711 levels. The stock price duly declined to this target level.

Trade Summary

- Initiate sell trade at ₹783 levels.
- Profit booking at the price target levels of ₹711 would have resulted in a profit of 72 points.

~

Example 9.13: IOC

In the case of Figure 9.13, Elliott Wave Theory suggests selling as and when the level of the bottom of Wave A is cracked on the downside during the down move from Wave B to Wave C. In other words, selling when the stock falls to around ₹309.75 levels. The stop loss is to be placed above the top of Wave B, i.e. at about ₹329 levels.

Fibonacci relationships would suggest the bottom of Wave 4, i.e. ₹275 levels, as the downside target. The stock price, however, did not fall to the target level and instead started rallying back up. During this rally a new wave pattern emerged in the form of an advancing Wave 3 at ₹309 levels, whereupon one should close all sell side positions.

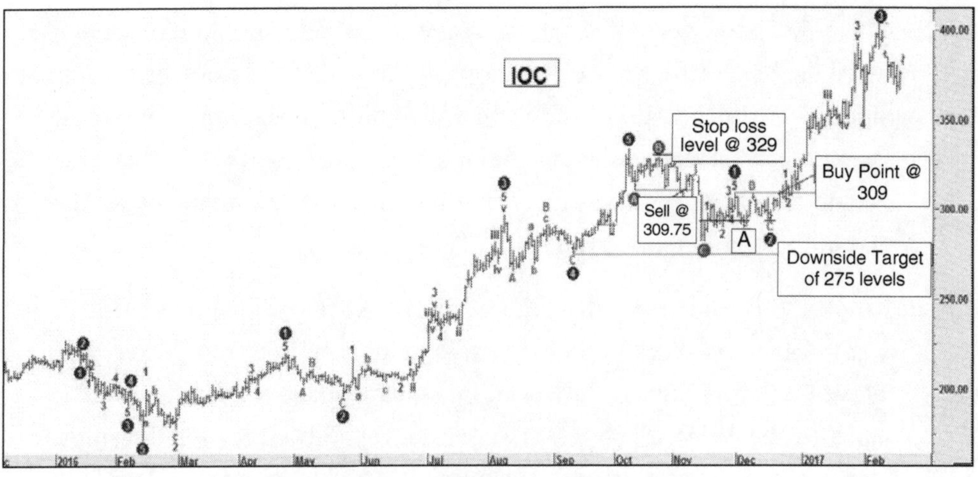

Figure 9.13: **Daily stock price chart of IOC**

~

Trade Summary

- Initiate sell trade at ₹309.75 levels.
- Profit booking at ₹309 levels on the downside would result in a profit of 0.75 points.

Buying When Wave 5 Ends in a Declining Market

Rules

- Buy as and when the level of fractal iv made during the earlier decline of Wave 5 is cracked on the upside. Before buying, however, one must make sure that the price is close to the Wave 5 target suggested by Fibonacci relationships, else the chances of a price rally diminishes. The buy trade stop loss should be placed below the lows of

Wave 5. The target is the top of Wave 4, i.e. one should exit as and when the price rallies to near the top of Wave 4. If the stock price falls short of this upside target, and starts declining instead, then one must keep an eye on the new wave count which might emerge at that time — and exit accordingly — because a new wave count might signal the end of the ongoing price rally.

- Else, buy as and when the high of Wave A, formed after the downward Wave 5 is cracked on the upside in an up move from Wave B to Wave C. Before buying, however, one must make sure that the price is close to the Wave 5 target as suggested by Fibonacci relationships, else the chances of a price rally diminish. The buy trade stop loss is to be placed below the lows of Wave B. Thereafter, one should use the Fibonacci relationship study for predicting the target for Wave C. Most times, Wave C halts at around the top of Wave 4, in which case the trader should close the long position by booking profit at that point. If the stock price falls short of the upside target and starts declining instead, the trader needs to keep an eye on the new wave count which might then emerge — and exit accordingly. This is because a new wave count might signal the end of the ongoing price rally.

Let's understand these rules better with the help of some real examples from the Indian stock market.

~

Example 9.14: Arvind Ltd

In the case of Figure 9.14, Elliott Wave Theory would suggest buying as and when the stock price subsequently closes above the highs of the preceding Wave 1, i.e. buying at around ₹285 levels. The stop loss is to be placed below the bottom of Wave 2, i.e. at about ₹257 levels, to protect against any unexpected downside. Most times when buying at the end of

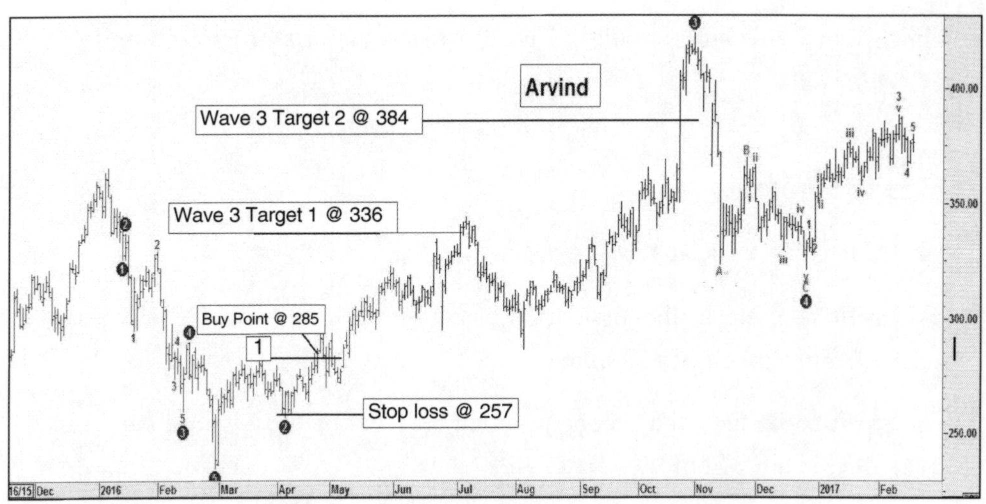

Figure 9.14: **Daily stock price chart of Arvind Ltd**

~

the declining Wave 5, the upside target is around the top of Wave 4. However, if the buying level is either above the top of Wave 4 — i.e. above the target level, — or a little below the top of Wave 4 — i.e. a little below the target level — then one must make use of Fibonacci relationships for determining the price target. Here, Fibonacci relationships suggest the following:

- The first price target level for Wave 3 is ₹336, i.e. at 1.618 times the length of Wave 1;
- The second price target level for Wave 3 is ₹384, i.e. at 2.618 times the length of Wave 1.

Experience suggests that when the buying level is either above the top of Wave 4, or a little below the top of Wave 4, then one must exit the long position by booking profit at the second price target level. This is because stock prices often demonstrate a sharp decline after rallying to the second price target levels.

In this case, the stock price did indeed reach the second price target of ₹384 levels.

Trade Summary

- Initiate buy trade at ₹285 levels.
- Profit booking at the first price target level of ₹336 would have resulted in a profit of 51 points.
- Profit booking at the second price target level of ₹384 would have resulted in a profit of 99 points.

~

Example 9.15: Indiabulls Real Estate

In the case of Figure 9.15, Elliott Wave Theory would suggest buying as and when the stock price subsequently closes above the highs of Wave A, i.e. buying at about ₹63.50 levels. The long trade stop loss can be placed below the bottom of Wave B, i.e. at levels of around ₹53.

Most times while buying at the end of a declining Wave 5, the upside price target is around the top of Wave 4. However, if the buying level is either above the top of Wave 4 — i.e. above the target level — or a little below the top of Wave 4 — i.e. a little below the target level, — then one must apply Fibonacci relationships for determining price targets. Here, the Fibonacci relationship study would suggest:

- The first price target level for Wave 3 is ₹78, i.e. at 1.618 times the length of Wave A;
- The second price target level for Wave 3 is ₹94, i.e. at 2.618 times the length of Wave A.

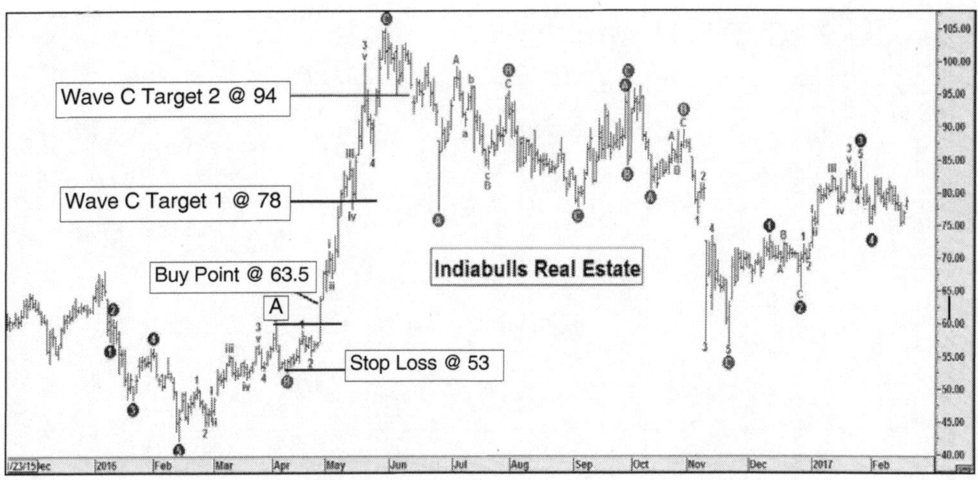

Figure 9.15: **Daily stock price chart of Indiabulls Real Estate**

~

Experience suggests that when the buying level is above the top of Wave 4, or a little below the top of Wave 4, then one must exit the long trade position by booking profit at the second price target level. This is because the stock price typically demonstrates a sharp decline after rallying up to the second price target levels.

In this case, the stock price rallied up to the second price target levels of ₹94.

Trade Summary

- Initiate buy trade at ₹63.50 levels.
- Profit booking at the first upside price target level of ₹78 would have resulted in a profit of 14.50 points.
- Profit booking at the second upside price target level of ₹94 would have resulted in a profit of 30.50 points.

Example 9.16: TVS Electronics

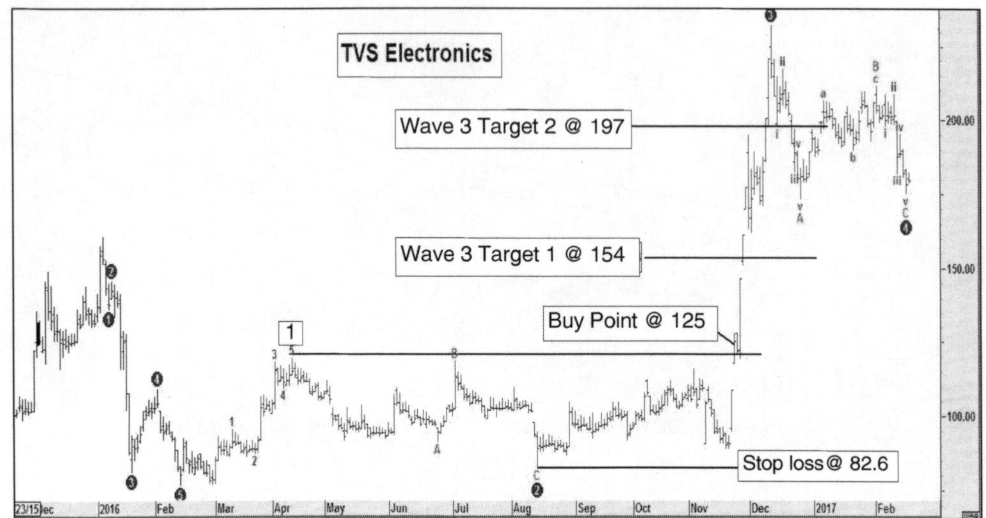

Figure 9.16: **Daily stock price chart of TVS Electronics**

~

In the case of Figure 9.16, Elliott Wave Theory would suggest buying as and when the stock price subsequently closes above the highs of the earlier Wave 1, i.e. buying at about ₹125 levels. The buy trade stop loss is to be placed below the bottom of Wave 2, i.e. at about ₹82.60 levels. Most times while buying at the end of a declining Wave 5, the upside price target is around the top of Wave 4. However, if the buying level is either above the top of Wave 4 — i.e. above the target level — or a little below the top of Wave 4 — i.e. a little below the target level — then one must use Fibonacci relationships for determining price targets. Here, the Fibonacci relationship study suggests:

- The first price target level for Wave 3 is ₹154, i.e. at 1.618 times the length of Wave 1;
- The second price target level for Wave 3 is ₹197, i.e. at 2.618 times the length of Wave 1.

Experience has shown that when the buying level is above top of Wave 4, or a little below the top of Wave 4, then one must exit the buy side position by booking profit at the second price target level. This is because stock prices often demonstrate a sharp decline after rallying up to the second price target levels.

In this case, the stock price did rally up to the second price target levels of ₹197.

Trade Summary

- Initiate buy trade at ₹125 levels.
- Profit booking at the first price target level of ₹154 would have resulted in a profit of 29 points.
- Profit booking at the second price target level of ₹197 would have resulted in a profit of 72 points.

~

Example 9.17: Zee Media

In the case of Figure 9.17, Elliott Wave Theory would suggest buying Zee Media as and when the stock price closes above the highs of the earlier Wave 1, in other words, buying at around ₹20.80 levels. The trade stop loss is to be placed below the bottom of Wave 2, i.e. at ₹18.25 levels to protect against any unexpected downside. Most times while buying at the end a declining Wave 5, the upside price target is around the top of Wave 4. However, if the buying level is either above the top of Wave 4, i.e. above the target level — or a little below the top of Wave 4, i.e. a little below the target level, — then one must make use of Fibonacci

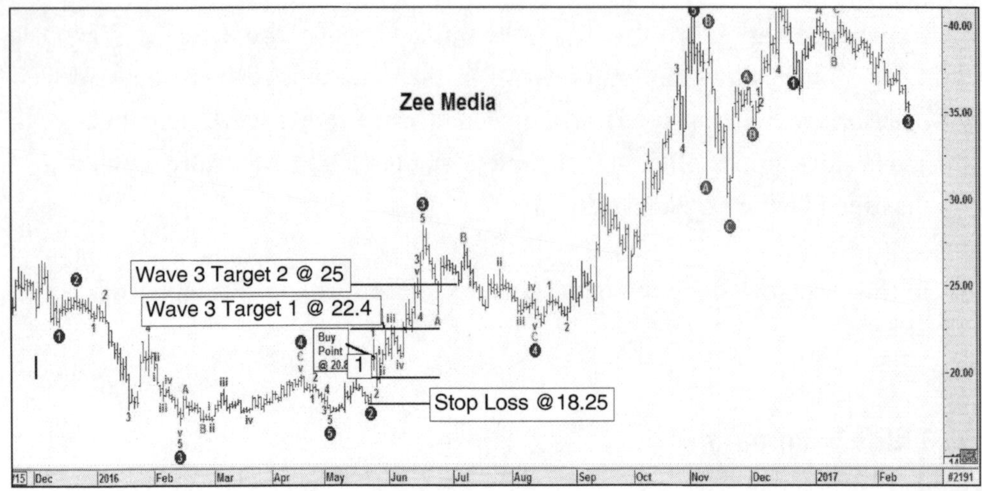

Figure 9.17: **Daily stock price chart of Zee Media**

~

relationships for arriving at price targets. Here, the Fibonacci relationship study would suggest:

- The first price target level for Wave 3 is ₹22.40, i.e. at 1.618 times the length of Wave 1;
- The second price target level for Wave 3 is ₹25, i.e. at 2.618 times the length of Wave 1.

Experience suggests that when the buying level is either above the top of Wave 4, or a little below the top of Wave 4, then one must exit the buy side positions by booking profit at the second price target level. This is because stock prices typically demonstrate sharp declines after rallying up to the second price target level.

In this case, the stock price rallied up to the second price target level of ₹25.

Trade Summary

- Initiate buy trade at ₹20.80 levels.
- Profit booking at the first upside price target levels of ₹22.40 would have resulted in a profit of 1.60 points.
- Profit booking at the second upside price target levels of ₹25 would have resulted in a profit of 4.20 points.

~

Example 9.18: Adani Power

In the case of Figure 9.18, Elliott Wave Theory would suggest buying as and when the stock price closes above the highs of Wave 1, i.e. buying around levels of ₹27.25. The stop loss would be placed below the bottom of Wave 2, i.e. at around ₹23.65 levels. Most times while buying at the end of a declining Wave 5, the upside price target is around the top of Wave 4, i.e. at around ₹31.40 levels in this case.

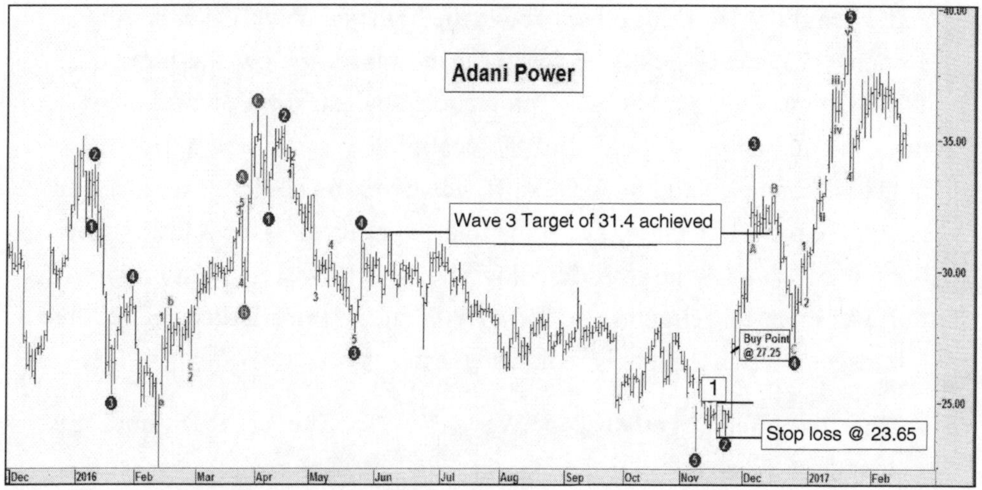

Figure 9.18: **Daily stock price chart of Adani Power**

~

Experience suggests that one must exit buy side positions whenever the price reaches the target which is the top of Wave 4 because most times the stock prices undergo a sharp correction after rallying to the top of Wave 4.

Here, the stock price duly rallied to the target levels of ₹31.40.

Trade Summary

- Initiate buy trade at ₹27.50 levels.
- Profit booking at the target price level of the ₹31.40 would have resulted in a profit of 4.15 points.

~

Example 9.19: Ashiana Housing

In the case of Figure 9.19, Elliott Wave Theory would suggest buying as and when the stock price closes above the highs of Wave 1, i.e. buying at around ₹173 levels. The stop loss is to be placed below the bottom of Wave 2, i.e. at ₹137 levels as protection against any downside. Most times while buying at the end of the declining Wave 5, the upside price target is around the top of Wave 4. If, however, the buying level is either above the top of Wave 4, i.e. above the target level — or a little below the top of Wave 4, i.e. a little below the target level — then one must turn to Fibonacci relationships for arriving at the price targets. Here, the Fibonacci relationship study would suggest:

- The first price target level for Wave 3 is ₹167, i.e. at 1.618 times the length of Wave 1;
- The second price target level for Wave 3 is ₹185, i.e. at 2.618 times the length of Wave 1.

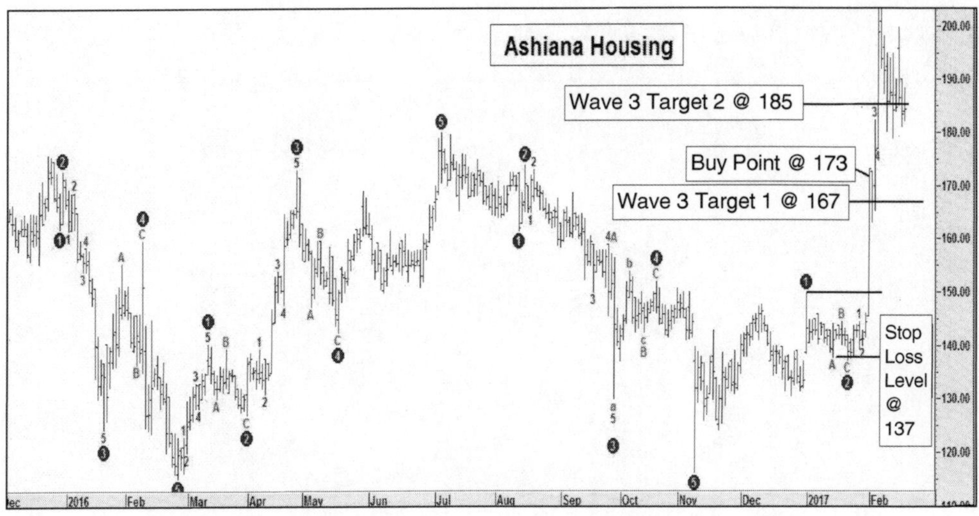

Figure 9.19: **Daily stock price chart of Ashiana Housing**

~

Since the first price target of ₹167 is below the buying price of ₹173, it should be ignored in this case.

Experience suggests that when the buying level is above the top of Wave 4, or a little below the top of Wave 4, then one must exit the buy position by booking profit at the second price target level because stock prices often decline sharply after rallying to the second upside price target level.

Here, the stock price rallied to the second upside price target level of around ₹185.

Trade Summary

- Initiate buy trade at ₹173 levels.
- Profit booking at the first upside price target level at ₹185 would have resulted in a profit of 12 points.

Example 9.20: Assam Company

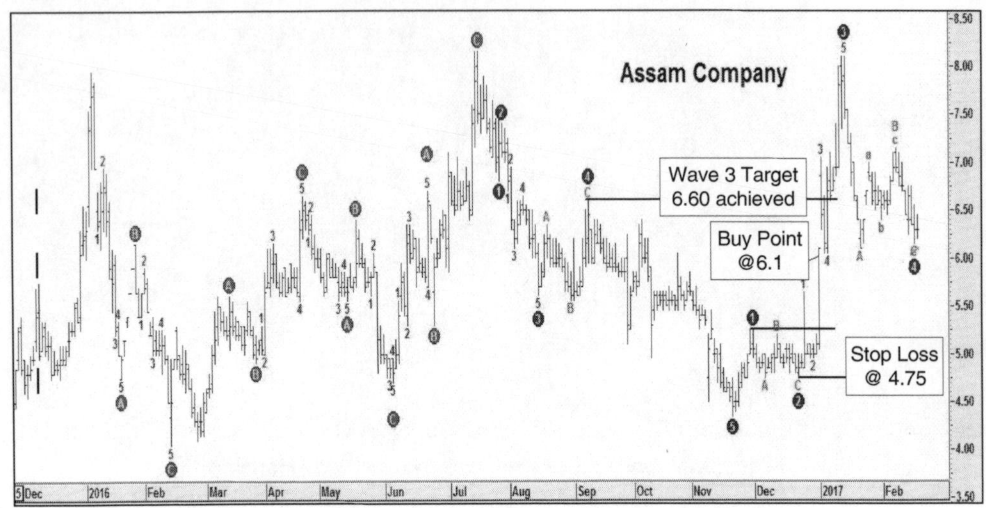

Figure 9.20: **Daily stock price chart of Assam Company**

~

In the case of Figure 9.20, Elliott Wave Theory suggests buying as and when the stock price subsequently closes above the highs of the earlier Wave 1, i.e. buying at around ₹6.10 levels. The stop loss is to be placed below the bottom of Wave 2, i.e. at levels of ₹4.75. Most times while buying at the end of a declining Wave 5, the upside price target is around the top of Wave 4, i.e. around ₹6.60 levels in this case.

Experience suggests that one must exit long positions whenever the price reaches the top of Wave 4 target. This is so because most times stock prices demonstrate a sharp correction after rallying to the top of Wave 4.

In this instance, the stock price rallied to the price target of around ₹6.60 levels on the upside.

Trade Summary

- Initiate buy trade at ₹6.10 levels.
- Profit booking at the first upside price target level of ₹6.60 would have resulted in a profit of 0.50 points.

~

Example 9.21: Future Retail

In the case of Figure 9.21, Elliott Wave Theory suggests buying as and when the stock price closes above the highs of Wave 1, i.e. buying at about ₹148 levels in this instance. The stop loss is to be placed below the bottom of Wave 2, i.e. at around ₹120 levels. Most times while buying at the end of a declining Wave 5, the upside price target is around the top of Wave 4. However, if the buying level is either above the top of Wave 4, i.e. above the target level — or a little below the top of Wave 4, i.e.

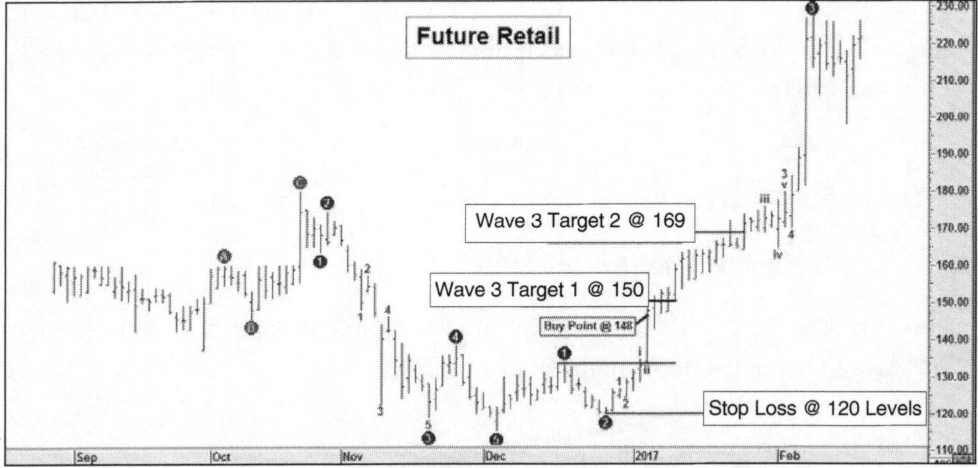

Figure 9.21: **Daily stock price chart of Future Retail**

~

a little below the target level — then one must make use of Fibonacci relationships for determining price targets. In this instance, Fibonacci relationship study would suggest:

- The first price target level for Wave 3 is ₹150, i.e. at 1.618 times the length of Wave 1;
- The second price target level for Wave 3 is ₹169, i.e. at 2.618 times the length of Wave 1.

In this case, since the first price target level of ₹150 is just above the buying price of ₹148, one should not buy for this first price target level of ₹150.

Experience suggests that when the buying level is either above the top of Wave 4, or a little below the top of Wave 4, then one must exit the buy position by booking profit at the second price target level. This is so because stock prices often decline sharply after rallying to the second upside price target levels.

Here, the stock price rallied up to the second price target level of around ₹169.

Trade Summary

- Initiate buy trade Buy at ₹148 levels.
- Profit booking at the second upside price target level of around ₹169 would have resulted in a profit of 21 points.

~

Example 9.22: Future Enterprises

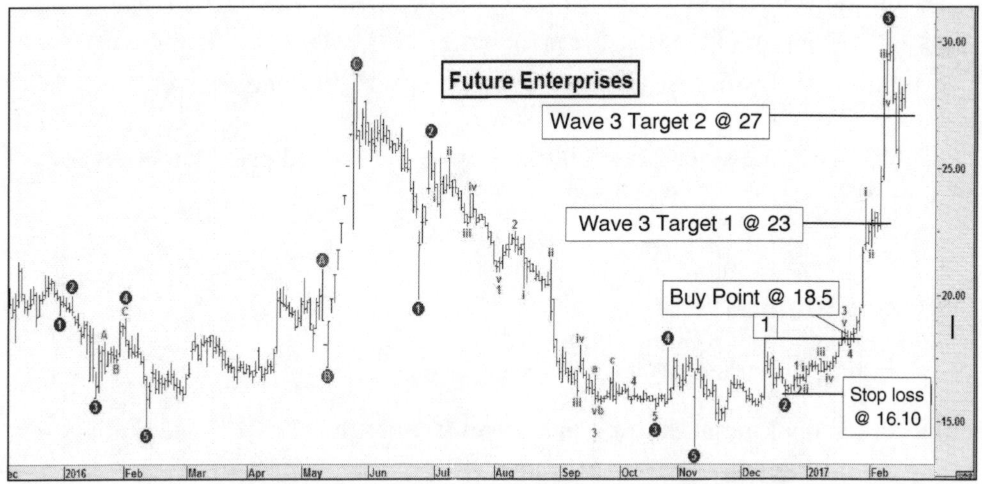

Figure 9.22: **Daily stock price chart of Future Enterprises**

~

In the case of Figure 9.22, Elliott Wave Theory suggests buying as and when the stock price closes above the highs of Wave 1, i.e. buying at around ₹18.50 levels in this case. The stop loss is to be placed below the bottom of Wave 2, i.e. at levels of about ₹16.10. Most times while buying at the end of the declining Wave 5, the upside price target is around the top of Wave 4. However, if the buying level is either above the top of Wave 4, i.e. above the target level — or a little below the top of Wave 4, i.e. a little below the target level, — then one can apply Fibonacci relationships for arriving at price targets. In this particular case, the Fibonacci relationship study would suggest the following:

- The first price target level for Wave 3 is ₹23, i.e. at 1.618 times the length of Wave 1;
- The second price target level for Wave 3 is ₹27, i.e. at 2.618 times the length of Wave 1.

Experience suggests that when the buying level is above the top of Wave 4, or a little below the top of Wave 4, then one must exit the long position by booking profit at the second price target level because stock prices often decline sharply after rallying to the second upside price target levels.

In this case, the stock price did rally up to the second price target levels of ₹27.

Trade Summary

- Initiate buy trade at ₹18.50 levels.
- Profit booking at the first upside price target level of ₹23 would have resulted in a profit of 4.50 points.
- Profit booking at the second upside price target level of ₹27 would have resulted in a profit of 8.50 points.

~

Example 9.23: Future Consumer Ltd

In the case of Figure 9.23, Elliott Wave Theory would suggest buying as and when the stock price closes above the highs of Wave 1, i.e. buying at around ₹23 levels. The stop loss is to be placed below the bottom of Wave 2, i.e. at ₹20.65 levels, to protect against any downside. Most times while buying at the end of the declining Wave 5, the upside price target is around the top of Wave 4. However, if the buying level is either above the top of Wave 4, i.e. above the target level — or a little below the top of Wave 4, i.e. a little below the target level — then one can consider Fibonacci relationships for arriving at price targets. Here the Fibonacci relationship study suggests:

- The first price target level for Wave 3 is ₹26, i.e. at 1.618 times the length of Wave 1;

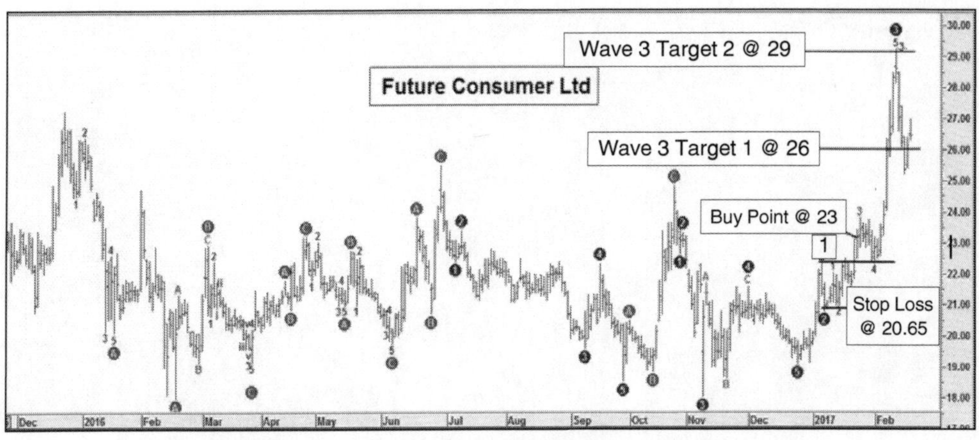

Figure 9.23: **Daily stock price chart of Future Consumer Ltd**

~

- The second price target level for Wave 3 is ₹29, i.e. at 2.618 times the length of Wave 1.

Experience has shown that when the buying level is above the top of Wave 4, or a little below the top of Wave 4, then one must exit the long position by booking profit at the second price target level. This is so because stock prices can demonstrate sharp declines after rallying to the price target levels.

In this case, the stock price rallied to the second upside price target level of ₹29.

Trade Summary

- Initiate buy trade at around ₹23 levels.
- Profit booking at the first upside price target level of ₹26 would have resulted in a profit of 3 points.
- Profit booking at the second upside price target level of ₹29 would have resulted in a profit of 6 points.

Example 9.24: BEML

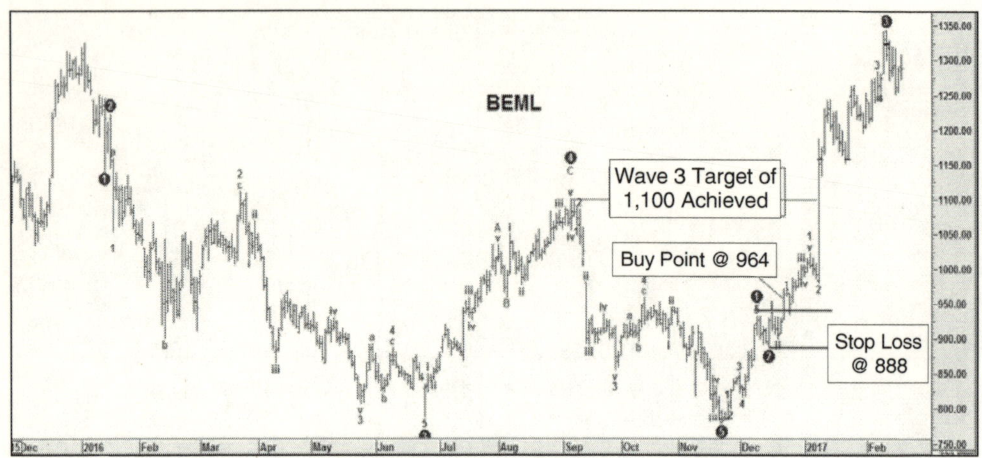

Figure 9.24: **Daily stock price chart of BEML**

~

In the case of Figure 9.24, Elliott Wave Theory would suggest buying as and when the stock price closes above the highs of Wave 1, i.e. buying at about ₹964 levels. The stop loss should be placed below the bottom of Wave 2, i.e. at about ₹888 levels. Most times while buying at the end of a declining Wave 5, the upside price target is around the top of Wave 4, i.e. around ₹1,100 levels in this case.

Experience suggests that one must exit long positions whenever the price target is the top of Wave 4. This is because most times stock prices show a sharp correction after rallying to the top of Wave 4.

Here the stock price rallied up to the target price levels of ₹1,100.

Trade Summary

- Initiate buy trade at ₹964 levels.
- Profit booking at the price target level of ₹11,000 would have resulted in a profit of 136 points.

~

Example 9.25: Blue Star

In the case of Figure 9.25, Elliott Wave Theory suggests buying as and when the stock price closes above the highs of Wave 1, i.e. buying at ₹358 levels. Here the stop loss is to be placed below the bottom of Wave 2, i.e. at about ₹323 levels. Usually while buying at the end a declining Wave 5, the price target is around the top of Wave 4. However, if the buying level is either above the top of Wave 4, i.e. above the target

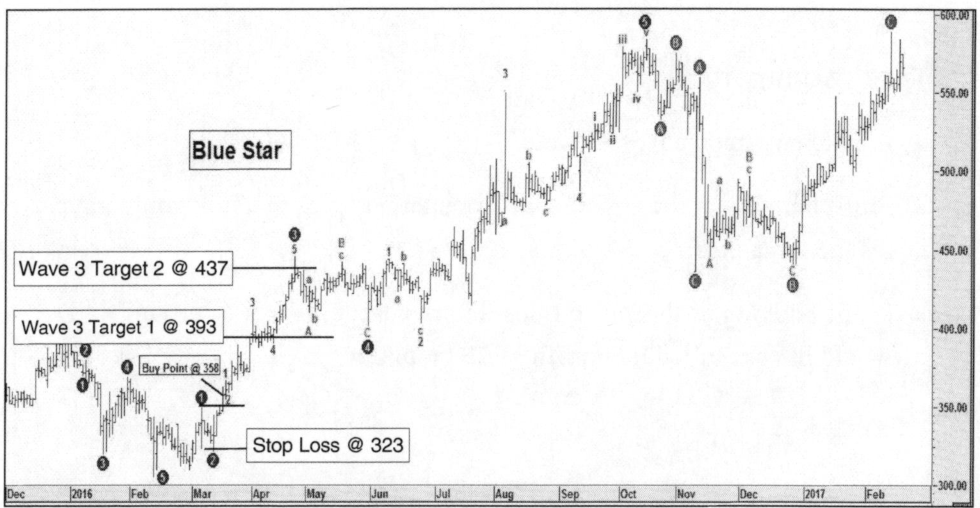

Figure 9.25: **Daily stock price chart of Blue Star**

~

level — or a little below the top of Wave 4, i.e. a little below the target level, one can use Fibonacci relationships for setting price targets. In this case, the Fibonacci relationship study would suggest:

- The first price target level for Wave 3 of ₹393, i.e. at 1.618 times the length of Wave 1;
- The second price target level for Wave 3 of ₹437, i.e. at 2.618 times the length of Wave 1.

Experience suggests that when the buying level is above the top of Wave 4, or a little below the top of Wave 4, one must exit the buy side position by booking profit at the second price target level. This is because stock prices often show a sharp decline after rallying up to the second price target levels.

Here, the stock price duly rallied to the second price target of around ₹437 level.

Trade Summary

- Initiate buy trade at ₹358 levels.
- Profit booking at the first upside price target level of ₹392 would have resulted in a profit of 34 points.
- Profit booking at the second upside price target levels of around ₹437 would have resulted in a profit of 79 points.

~

Example 9.26: Bombay Burmah

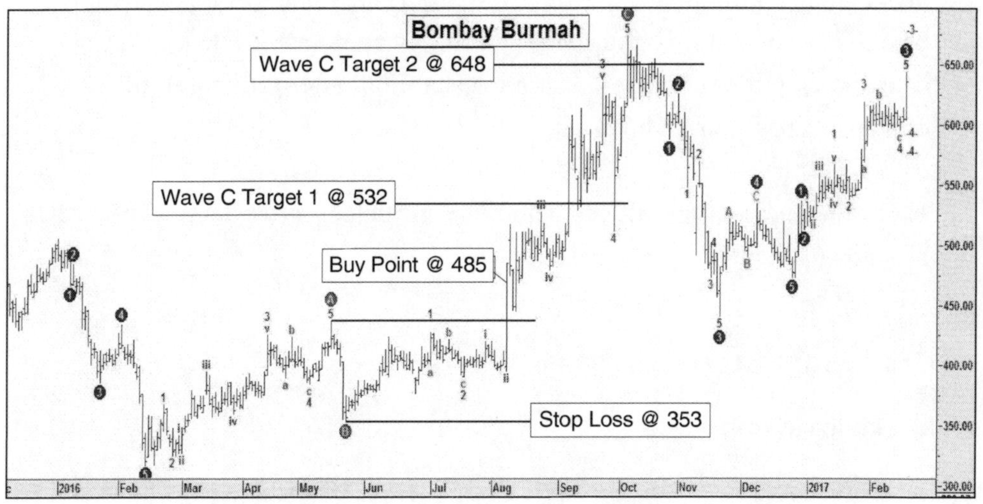

Figure 9.26: **Daily stock price chart of Bombay Burmah**

~

In the case of Figure 9.96, Elliott Wave Theory suggests buying as and when the stock price closes above the highs of Wave A, i.e. buying at ₹485 levels. The stop loss can be placed below the bottom of Wave B, i.e. at around ₹353 levels, in order to protect against any unexpected down move. Most times while buying at the end a declining Wave 5, the upside price target is around the top of Wave 4. However if the buying level is either above the top of Wave 4, i.e. above the target level — or a little below the top of Wave 4, i.e. just a little below the target level — then one can use Fibonacci relationships for setting price targets. Here, the Fibonacci relationship study would suggest:

- The first price target level for Wave C of ₹532, i.e. at 1.618 times the length of Wave A;
- The second price target level for Wave C of ₹648, i.e. at 2.618 times the length of Wave A.

Experience suggests that when the buying level is either above the top of Wave 4, or a little below the top of Wave 4, then one must exit the buy position by booking profit at the second price target level. This is because stock prices often demonstrate a sharp fall after rallying to the second upside price target level.

Here, the stock price rallied to the second upside price target level of around ₹648 levels.

Trade Summary

- Buying at ₹485 levels.
- Profit booking at the first price target level of ₹532 would have resulted in a profit of 47 points.
- Profit booking at the second price target level of ₹648 would have resulted in a profit of 163 points.

~

Example 9.27: BPL

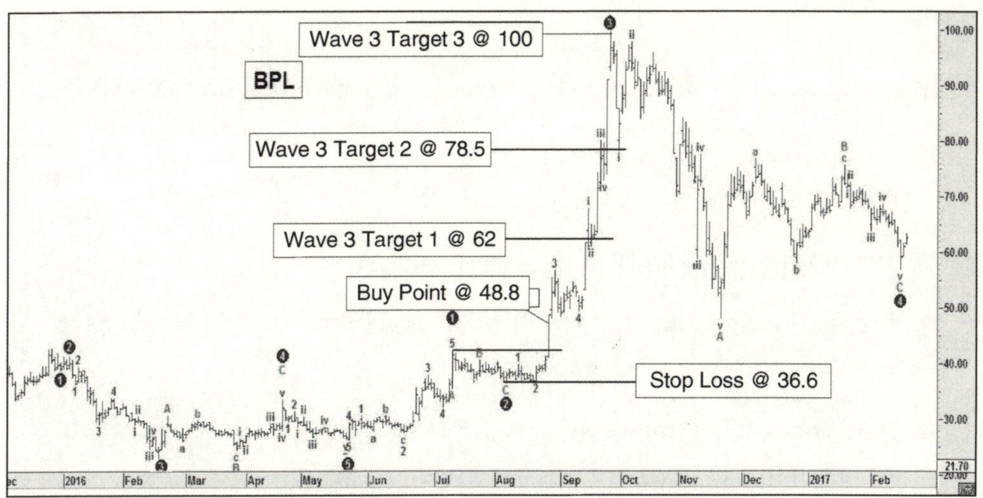

Figure 9.27: **Daily stock price chart of BPL**

~

In the case of Figure 9.27, Elliott Wave Theory suggests buying BPL as and when the stock price closes above the highs of Wave 1, i.e. buying at around ₹48.80 levels. The stop loss is to be placed below the bottom of Wave 2, i.e. at ₹36.60 levels. Most times while buying at the end of a declining Wave 5, the upside target is the top of Wave 4. But if buying level is above the top of Wave 4, as is the case in this example, then one should make use of Fibonacci relationships for determining price targets. I have learnt from my experience that most times the price target of 4.25 times the length of Wave 1 is achieved.

Here, the Fibonacci relationship study suggests:

- The first price target of ₹62 levels for Wave 3, i.e. at 1.618 times the length of Wave 1;
- The second price target of ₹78.50 levels for Wave 3, i.e. at 2.618 times the length of Wave 1;

- The third price target for Wave 3 is ₹100 levels, i.e. at 4.25 times the length of Wave 1.

Actually, the stock price rallied up to the third price target level of ₹100.

Trade Summary

- Buying at ₹48.80 levels.
- Profit booking at the first upside price target levels of ₹62 would have resulted in a profit of 13.20 points.
- Profit booking at the second upside price target level of ₹78.50 would have resulted in a profit of 29.70 points.
- Profit booking at the third upside price target level of ₹100 would have resulted in a profit of 51.20 points.

~

Example 9.28: Brooks Laboratories

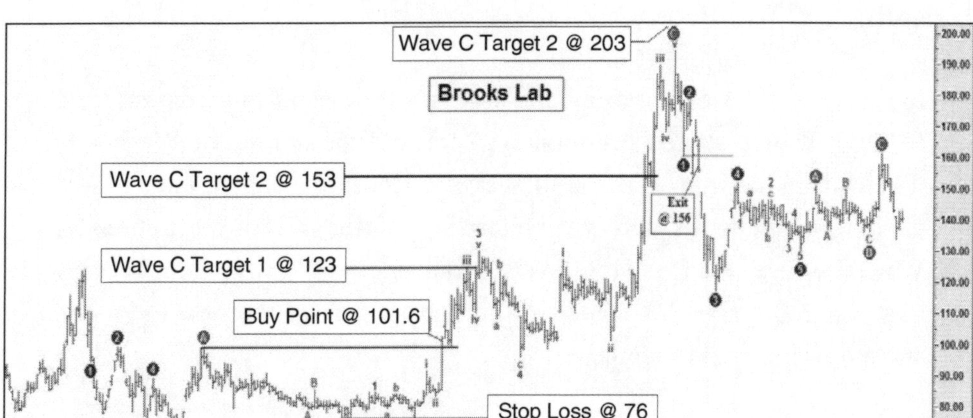

Figure 9.28: **Daily stock price chart of Brooks Laboratories**

~

In the case of Figure 9.28, Elliott Wave Theory suggests buying as and when the stock price of Brooks Laboratories closes above the highs of Wave 1, i.e. buying at around ₹101.60 levels. The stop loss can be placed below the bottom of Wave 2, i.e. at ₹76 levels. Most times while buying at the end of a declining Wave 5, the upside target is the top of Wave 4. However, if the buying level is either above the top of Wave 2, or a little below the top of Wave 2, then one must make use of the Fibonacci relationship study to set the price target and one must hold the buy side positions for the aggressive price target of 4.25 times the length of Wave C. In case this aggressive price target is not achieved, one can exit as per then the prevailing wave count. Here, Fibonacci relationships suggest:

- The first price target level for Wave C is ₹123, i.e. at 1.618 times the length of Wave 1;
- The second price target level for Wave C is ₹153, i.e. at 2.618 times the length of Wave 1; and

- The third price target level for Wave C is ₹203, i.e. at 4.25 times the length of Wave 1.

In this case, the stock price stopped rising a little short of the target level of ₹203. It then started declining and cracked the bottom of Wave 1 in the down move from Wave 2 to Wave 3. Here, one should have closed all long positions as and when the price closed below the bottom of Wave 1 — i.e. at about ₹156 levels during the down move from Wave 2 to Wave 3 because this signalled that the up move has come to an end and a down move is in force.

Trade Summary

- Buying at ₹101.60 levels.
- Profit booking at the first price target level of ₹123 on the upside would have resulted in a profit of 21.40 points.
- Profit booking at the second price target level of ₹153 on the upside would have resulted in a profit of 51.40 points.
- Closing the buy side position at the exit point, i.e. at ₹156 levels, would have resulted in a profit of 54.40 points.

~

Example 9.29: Apollo Tyre

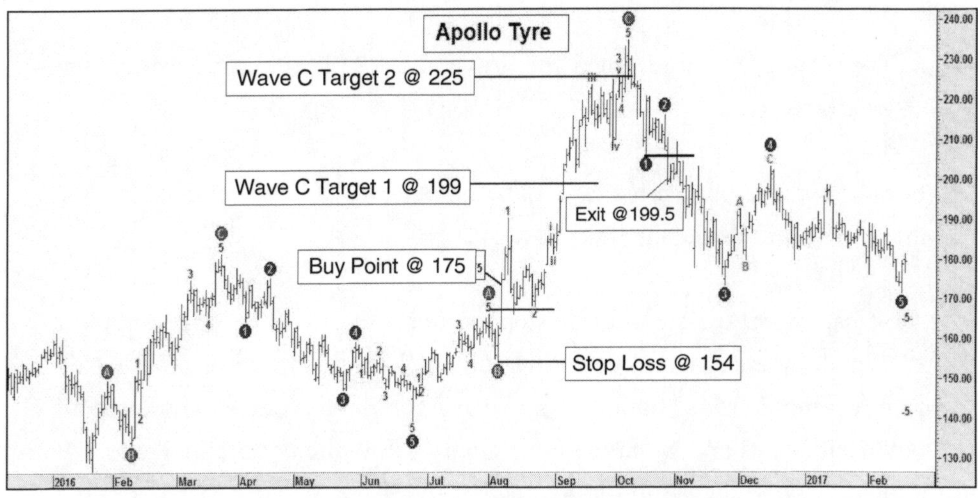

Figure 9.29: **Daily stock price chart of Apollo Tyre**

~

In the case of Figure 9.29, Elliott Wave Theory suggests buying as and when the stock price closes above the highs of Wave 1, i.e. buying at around ₹175 levels. In this case the stop loss should be placed below the bottom of Wave 2, i.e. at about ₹154 levels, to protect against any unexpected down move. Most times while buying at the end of a declining Wave 5, the upside target is the top of Wave 4. But if the buying level is above the top of Wave 4, as is the case in this example, then one must make use of Fibonacci relationships for determining price targets. I have learnt from experience that in such situations the price target of 4.25 times the length of Wave 1 usually achieved.

Here, Fibonacci relationships would suggest:

- The first price target level for Wave C is ₹199, i.e. at 1.618 times the length of Wave 1;

- The second price target level for Wave C is ₹225, i.e. at 2.618 times the length of Wave 1;
- The third price target level for Wave C is ₹272, i.e. at 4.25 times the length of Wave 1.

In this case, the third price target level around ₹272 is not marked in Figure 9.29 as it falls outside the chart's range.

As it happened, the stock price stopped rising short of the price target of ₹272 and, instead, started declining and cracked the bottom of Wave 1 on its down move from Wave 2 to Wave 3. Accordingly, one should close all buy positions as and when the price closes below the bottom of Wave 1 at around ₹199.50 levels during its down move from Wave 2 to Wave 3 because this signals that the up move has come to an end and a down move is in force.

Trade Summary

- Buying at ₹175 levels.
- Profit booking at the first upside price target level of ₹199 would have resulted in a profit of 24 points.
- Profit booking at the second upside price target level of ₹225 would have resulted in a profit of 50 points.
- Closing the buy side position at the exit point, at ₹199.50 level would result in a profit of 24.50 points.

~

Example 9.30: TVS Srichakra

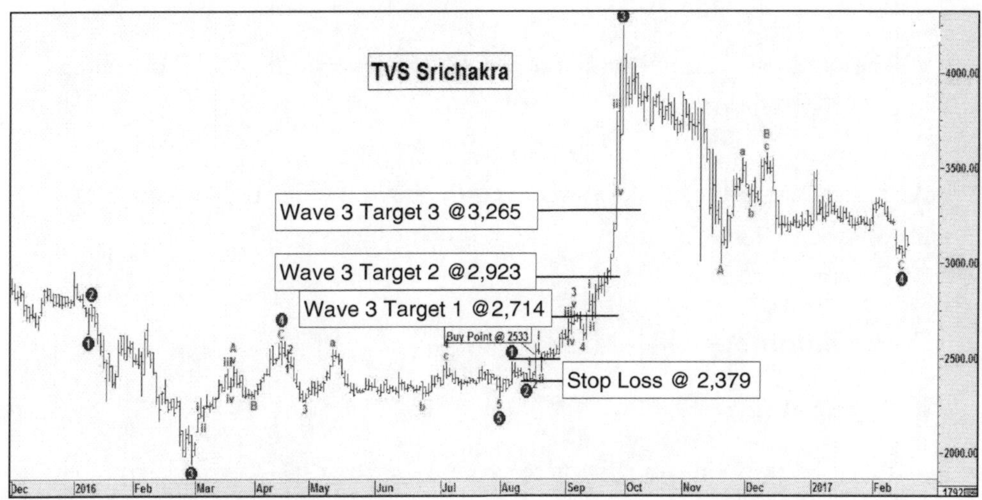

Figure 9.30: **Daily stock price chart of TVS Srichakra**

~

In the case of Figure 9.30, Elliott Wave Theory suggests buying as and when the stock price closes above the highs of Wave 1, i.e. buying at around ₹2,533 levels. The stop loss is to be placed below the bottom of Wave 2, i.e. at ₹2,379 levels.

Most times while buying at the end of a declining Wave 5, the upside targets are the top of Wave 4. If, however, the declining Wave 5 falls short of the target, then one must make use of Fibonacci relationships for forecasting price targets which would suggest holding the buy positions for the aggressive price target of 4.25 times the length of Wave 1. Should this aggressive price target not be achieved, one should exit as per the then prevailing wave count. Here, the Fibonacci relationship study suggests:

- The first price target for Wave 3 is ₹2,714 levels, i.e. at 1.618 times the length of Wave 1;

- The second price target for Wave 3 is of ₹2,923 levels, i.e. at 2.618 times the length of Wave 1;
- The third price target for Wave 3 is ₹3,265 levels, i.e. at 4.25 times the length of Wave 1.

As it turned out, the stock price rallied to above the third price target levels of around 3,265.

Trade Summary

- Buying at ₹2,533 levels.
- Profit booking at the first price target level of ₹2,714 would have resulted in a profit of 181 points.
- Profit booking at the second price target level of ₹2,923 would have resulted in a profit of 390 points.
- Profit booking at the third price target of ₹3,265 would have resulted in a profit of 732 points.

~

10

Rebutting Critics of Elliott Wave Theory

- **Criticism:** As per Efficient Market Theory (EMT), stock prices cannot be predicted using past price and volume data.

  Rebuttal: No science, be it fundamental or technical analysis — and absolutely nothing in this universe — can predict stock market movements with complete certainty. By this yardstick, Elliott Wave Theory is at par with any other studies or theories.

- **Criticism:** If the top hundred Elliott Wave practitioners were gathered in a room, they would fail to reach a consensus on either the wave count or the direction in which a stock is headed. Critics also point out that using Elliott Wave Theory is more an art based on the subjective judgment of an analyst.

  Rebuttal: Elliott Wave trading is indeed an art and not a precise science where 2+2 always equals 4. In Elliott Wave trading, 2+2 has the potential of becoming any number, whether it be 0, 22, 100, depending upon how good you are in identifying Elliott Wave patterns

- **Criticism:** Elliott Wave Theory does not identify a wave at its very beginning, i.e. it does not facilitate buying at the bottom and selling at the top.

  Rebuttal: It is true that a wave is identified when some distance has already been covered but no other stock market theory, be it fundamental analysis or derivatives study, etc., ensures buying at the very bottom and selling at the very top. In fact, nobody can consistently buy at the bottom and sell at the top. Elliott Wave Theory is not the only theory or study to be faulted on this basis.

- **Criticism:** The stop loss is deep at the time of initiating a trade based on Elliott Wave Theory.

  Rebuttal: The stop loss is indeed deep but it's deep only at the time of initiating a trade, i.e. the risk is maximum only at the time of entering into a trade. Thereafter, in most cases, as and when the stock price moves in a favourable direction, the stop loss too narrows to a comfortable level. It is also true that a stop loss placed at the time of initiating a trade gets triggered without narrowing down to a comfortable level, but such instances are fewer. One can easily work out the proportion of instances where the initial stop loss placed at the time of trade initiation got triggered from the one hundred real examples given in this book.

- **Criticism:** Elliott Wave is only a popular theory but not a valid one.

  Rebuttal: There are no hundred per cent guarantees in the stock market. Stock markets are not the place for anyone looking for guaranteed profits.

To conclude, I would say that Elliott Wave Theory is indeed a good way of profitable trading in the stock market. In this book, I have supported this claim with one hundred real examples from the Indian stock market. As the saying goes, "The proof of the pudding lies in its eating."

~